Rob Reimer has written an important book for the church in our time. Many of the problems we face as disciples of Jesus and church leaders exist because we do not understand the authority we have in Christ. In this theological and thoughtful book, filled with rich practical implication, Rob empowers us to become the kind of disciples that Jesus had in mind.

—**JON TYSON**, *Lead Pastor of Church of the City New York and Author of "Beautiful Resistance"*

First of all, I am deeply moved that my dear friend, Rob, would dedicate a book to me. Secondly, I am even more deeply honored that he would choose to do so with this book on *Spiritual Authority*. As always, Rob brings us heavenly truth with earthly wisdom and clarity. The genius of this book is that authority is more than just positional! Anyone can grow in it and develop it. The lessons unpacked in *Spiritual Authority* hold the key for breakthrough for leaders, churches, and regions. Come Holy Spirit!

—**DR. RON WALBORN**, *Vice President and Dean of Nyack College and Alliance Theological Seminary*

In matters of the human heart and soul, in matters of the work of the Spirit, Dr. Rob Reimer brings insights that are rare in the 21st century. As a leader and pastor for 25 years, a graduate school professor, and an international speaker on the care of the soul, he brings depth, wisdom, and profound insights into leading out of a place of spiritual authority.

—**MARTIN SANDERS**, *founder of Global Leadership Inc, Director of the Doctoral Program at Alliance Theological Seminary.*

Spiritual Authority is yet another seminal work by Rob Reimer for those embracing and ministering in our Christ given authority as ministers of grace. In this book Rob Reimer has brought Biblical patterns, applicable principles and personal insights into how we walk in, and exercise, our spiritual authority in the power and presence of the Holy Spirit. He writes as one who has pursued and wrestled with God and found keys to faith, intimacy with God and effective ministry. For the partisan, pupil, preacher or proclaimer of faith in Christ, this work challenges and encourages us to demonstrate the kingdom and to set captives free.

—REV. KEN GRAHAM, *President, Christian and Missionary Alliance of Australia*

Our world is full of disconnect, disillusionment and despair. Churches and organizations are trying to come up with new strategies, fads, and ways to connect but, with a few exceptions, are finding little success. In *Spiritual Authority*, Rob Reimer once again calls his readers to what really matters and with a depth of insight that will help transform the expectations and experience of so many Christians—especially those endeavoring to lead others. The secret to success in our Christian life exists. It's more of Jesus, more authority, more presence, more intimacy and a lot less of us. Rob's Biblical understanding and clear practical applications will be a gift to many just as *Soul Care* has impacted so many thousands around the globe. I'm really excited to see how God uses this book to draw people to him and for true impact for his kingdom.

—TIM MEIER, *Vice President for Development with the Christian and Missionary Alliance USA*

The books I read seem to fall into three categories: those I read once, those I read in whole or in part twice, and those I read and reread numerous times. Rob's book on spiritual authority will fall into this last category. My forty-plus years in ministry leadership have shown me that without true spiritual authority, my efforts are just that—*my* efforts. While God can use and has used my efforts, that which I most long to see occurs only as a result of a clear manifestation of God's presence and power. If you want to move far beyond "my efforts," I highly recommend Rob's *Spiritual Authority*. And for what it's worth, Rob models what he writes, and I like that—I really like that.

    —**DON COUSINS**, *Lead Pastor, Discovery Church*
    Orlando, FL

It is time to put on some weight! Not physical pounds but spiritual muscle. The author with surgical precision and prophetic courage calls followers of Jesus to cultivate an intimacy with God that expands their capacity to carry his presence. Spiritual authority is not about activating our human potential but about unleashing the supernatural power of God through us. Rob declares, "People of authentic spiritual authority carry an unmistakable gravitas (weightiness) that comes without control or reliance on human forcefulness." The opportunities for kingdom advance have never been greater but followers of Jesus must take hold of the spiritual authority given to them by Jesus and touch Heaven in order to change earth. This book is not optional but essential.

    —**REV. DR. DAVID HEARN**, *President of the Christian and*
    Missionary Alliance in Canada

My friend Rob Reimer often says to me, and I paraphrase, "You can have as much of Jesus as you want. But you must be willing to pay the price." I thought that statement was only in reference to His presence. I now realize that it also relates to the expansion of His authority in my life and ministry. Spiritual authority is about that. And, once again, Dr. Reimer gives the church a powerful tool to understanding the keys to the kingdom. Thank you, Rob.

—**KELVIN WALKER**, *Metro District Superintendent of the Christian and Missionary Alliance*

SPIRITUAL
AUTHORITY

Partnering with God to Release the Kingdom

Dr. Rob Reimer

Carpenter's Son Publishing

Spiritual Authority

© 2020 by Rob Reimer

Published by Carpenter's Son Publishing, Franklin, Tennessee

Published in association with Larry Carpenter of
Christian Book Services, LLC
www.christianbookservices.com

Edited by Robert Irvin

Cover Design by Darcy Reimer

Interior Layout Design by Suzanne Lawing

Printed in the United States of America

978-1-952025-00-6

ACKNOWLEDGMENTS

In some ways writing is a solitary endeavor. I spend a great deal of time thinking, creating, editing, shaping, and reworking a book. But the truth is no book is ever produced in isolation. So, I want to take time to sincerely thank those who have contributed to this project.

I am grateful, as always, first and foremost for my family. You have all been involved in my life as an author now—and I am grateful for your help! The writing process takes time and I am often less attentive to you when I am in the throes of writing. You sacrifice every time I create a new book, and you share in whatever fruit these books produce. Jen: we celebrate our thirtieth anniversary this year and it really does keep getting better. So grateful for you and for your willingness to share our lives with others in teaching and writing. Thanks for administering nearly everything in Renewal International— customer service, advertising, marketing, shipping, editing, and working book tables. And the other dozens of things that you do! Darcy, thanks for designing the book cover to this book and *Calm in the Storm*. You're a talented artist and it was fun to do it with you! Danielle and Courtney: thank you for helping me with audiobooks in 2019 and 2020—more to come! All of you have also been involved in packaging, shipping, and various other details of the book business! Craig, thanks for manning book tables and helping lug books all over with me. All of you, thanks for letting me do what God has called me to do and supporting me on the journey! I love you all.

Bob Irvin and Larry Carpenter: thank you for partnering with me in creating books. Larry, this is now the fifth book I have published with you and I am grateful for your expertise in the process. Bob, thanks for editing with excellence and encouragement! You've both been a pleasure to work with!

To my friends and students at Alliance Theological Seminary, thank you for letting me serve with you for nearly two decades. When I was 24 years old, the Lord told me I would teach in Seminary, and I began as an adjunct in my thirties, and now I have been here full-time for three years. I love ATS, and I am grateful that God has let me serve here with you. To all of my students, I have learned much of what I teach in these pages in the classrooms with you. I have learned more about deliverance ministry working with ATS students than anyplace else. You have been eager and hungry for the freedom and fullness of Christ.

To all of you who have read my previous books and have written to me, emailed me, messaged me, and spoken to me about how they have helped you—thank you! It has meant a lot to me and I have appreciated every kind word you have taken the precious time to communicate! Much thanks to you all.

DEDICATION

I dedicate this book to my dear friend, Dr. Ron Walborn. Almost twenty years ago, when I was pastor of South Shore Community Church, I called Martin Sanders and told him I wanted to do a Holy Spirit weekend. I wanted to teach on the things of the Spirit and then do a lab time where we could train and equip people to experience the things we taught about. We would teach about hearing God's voice and then give people time to get in groups and listen to the Lord for one another. We would teach people about how to pray for the sick and then we would release them to pray for each other. We would teach on being filled with the Spirit and then we would pray for people to be filled. Martin immediately said to me, "We need to invite Ron Walborn." We did. You came and I am so grateful you did! It has changed my life!

Your love for Jesus and passion for the kingdom has inspired me over and over. Watching you minister in the power of the Holy Spirit with sincere desire to see the Kingdom of God come has caused me to long for more! Your honesty has spurred me on to become more honest and vulnerable. You really are one of the most honest people l know; I love that about you, and I am convinced that is one of the reasons God uses you so much. And your humor has brightened my day more times than I can possibly recount. Even when I already know the story, and could tell it word for word, I find myself laughing so hard it is like I am hearing it for the first time!

I have a ton of great memories with you, but my favorite of all was our trip to Pittsburgh. It was one of the darkest seasons of my life and I called you to process the pain in my soul. I simply said, "I need a day with you." And you immediately responded, "Tell me when." Knowing how busy you were, and what a sacrifice it was to give up a day, meant the world to me. That day was the beginning of a turning point for me. It helped me climb out of a deep pit, and every time I think about it, I am moved to tears with gratitude for your life and friendship. I love you, friend!

CONTENTS

An Unequal Display
of Jesus' Power: Why
Authority Matters

Thankfully, there are places in the world where the church is doing fantastically well, especially in the Global South. There are churches in North America that are growing rapidly and reaching people for Christ. By and large, however, the church in the West is losing ground. Currently, only 40 percent of Americans are open to church. The percentage is far less in the Northeast, where I have spent my life.

The world has changed and, for the most part, the church is no longer effective at reaching the world we live in. I often feel as though seminaries are preparing people for ministry in a church that is no longer effective and for a world that no longer exists.

Alan Hirsch, in his book *The Forgotten Ways,* wrote, "The reality we deal with is that now, after some two thousand years of the gospel, Christianity is on the decline in every Western cultural context. In fact, in terms of percentage of the population, we are proportionately further away from getting the job done than we were at the end of the third century!"[1] What kind of church will it take to reach the 60 percent of Americans who are no longer interested in church? What kind of church leaders do we need today to turn this trend around?

Our world has shifted from a modern worldview to a postmodern worldview. We have moved from a society where truth was an absolute to a world where the dominant belief is that truth cannot be known. We have shifted from a society rooted in Judeo-Christian values to a post-Christian society. The church is rapidly declining and losing influence in society; our voice is no longer valued, and we are being marginalized. What was once considered a "Christian society" rooted in Christian values is now rapidly moving toward an anti-Christian bias. Europe went this path first, then Canada, and now the United States is following these worldview shifts.

Lesslie Newbigin was a British theologian, missiologist, and author; he died in 1998. He wrote with unusual insight about this shift that had taken place for Europe in his day, and for the American continent in our day. Newbigin said, "What we have is . . . a pagan society whose public life is ruled by beliefs which are false. And because it is not a pre-Christian paganism, but a paganism born out of the rejection of Christianity, it is far tougher and more resistant to the Gospel than the pre-Christian paganisms with which foreign missionaries have been in contact during the past two hundred years. Here, without possibility of question, is the most challenging missionary frontier of our time."[2] This is a brilliant insight. We are tasked with the mission of trying to reach people who are far from God because they have rejected Christianity.

The key is that they have rejected the version of Christianity that they were presented. They rejected the version of Christianity that I grew up in: a version that was often dogmatic and legalistic. They have turned away from an expression of Christianity that overemphasized truth and underemphasized love. They walked away from a brand of Christianity that was built more on precepts than on experiential reality. They dismissed a Christianity that, all too often, presented the gospel without a demonstration of power. In short, they didn't reject the Jesus of the Gospels that consistently moved in love and with demonstrations of heavenly power; they rejected *the Jesus that the church presented.* Truth is important, it is vital and necessary, but it must be delivered in love. Jesus was full of truth and full of grace.

It wasn't a tension or a balance. When He spoke in the fullness of truth, He never let go of the fullness of grace. Too often the world has perceived the church as being full of her version of the truth but lacking in grace. Precepts matter, but they must be demonstrated and validated by the power of God.

In many ways we are living in a day and age that is more similar to the New Testament cities of Corinth and Ephesus than we are to a world that resembles North America in 1950 or even 1980.

This is why I have plenty of hope: while people are closed to church, many are still open to Jesus. If Jesus walked in our neighborhoods today doing the ministry that we see Him doing in the gospels—healing the sick, casting out demons, teaching heavenly revelation—people would still flock to Him. While people today wonder if there is such a thing as a knowable version of absolute truth, they are open to spiritual experience and they believe in a spiritual world. In many ways we are living in a day and age that is more similar to the New Testament cities of Corinth and Ephesus than we are to a world that resembles North America in 1950 or even 1980. And those two ancient cities experienced a tremendous outpouring of the Spirit and massive amounts of people coming to faith in Christ.

What will it take to turn the church around and reach this generation? I think the answer is complex and varied. But it starts with life change. We need followers of Jesus who look like Jesus, act like Jesus, serve like Jesus, love like Jesus, and minister like Jesus. They will make Jesus attractive to this generation. We are His body, His hands, and His feet. This generation will not come to faith unless we represent Jesus well. We need to represent his heart for the hurting, the downtrodden, the oppressed, the poor, the hungry, and the disenfranchised. We need to move in the power of God to set captives free and bring hope to the hopeless, healing to the hurting, peace to the anxious, and love to those who have felt unlovable. This kind of lived-out faith will attract people who are not open to a church that was more known for truth than love, more known for precepts than power. When we carry the presence of Jesus to those around us, they will be drawn by His love and power. Whenever Jesus showed up in a community in the Gospels, people flocked to Him. Truth presented in love and demonstrated with power is winsome and represents Jesus well. When we show up with Jesus' presence in our communities today, they will come.

I believe soul care is a huge gateway to evangelism in this generation. I don't necessarily mean my book *Soul Care*—I mean the freedom and fullness that is available to people in Christ. I think more people are going to come to faith in Christ in this generation because they know they are broken and in need of a Healer than because they know they are sinners in need of a Savior. This is not a theological statement; this is a missiological statement. I am not saying they aren't sinners, that they don't need a Savior. I am saying that they likely don't know they are sinners in need of a Savior. And trying to convince them of this truth will not win them to Jesus. But they do know that they are broken. More people are struggling with anxiety than ever before; anxiety has recently passed depression as the number one mental health issue in the United States. People have real pain and are looking for real life solutions and hope, and if the church can learn how to minister Jesus' healing power to alleviate the pain and suffering people face, many will follow Jesus.

Healing can be a powerful gateway to discovering that someone is a sinner in need of a Savior. Read the Gospels. Jesus often attracts the crowds because of His healing ministry. That was true then, and it is true today. When we move in soul healing and in societal healing through compassionate justice issues, we will demonstrate Jesus' relevance and compassion to this generation. They will find Jesus irretrievably attractive. Jesus is the most beautiful, most compelling, most powerful person who ever lived. He is irresistibly attractive to people who encounter His risen presence.

> Jesus is the most beautiful, most compelling, most powerful person who ever lived. He is irresistibly attractive to people who encounter His risen presence.

In addition to having people who are transformed and living Christ-honoring, attractive lives, we need people who are mobilized on mission. If the leaders of the church get people in their churches free and full in Christ but don't mobilize those transformed people on mission, the church will not be effective in this society. And just because people get free and full does not mean they will automatically live on mission; they must be mobilized on mission by leaders who have the heart of God for their community.

The days are nearly gone when you could hang a shingle and expect people who had spiritual desire to show up at church. People who sense spiritual hunger aren't open to church, for the most part, so they aren't going to come. They will look to other options to satisfy their spiritual hunger. Hirsch, in his book *The Forgotten Ways*, talks about the fact that the 40 percent who are open to church is a rapidly shrinking crowd, and most of the churches that exist today are designed to compete for those 40 percent.[3] We need leaders to mobilize transformed people on mission so that we take Jesus and the gospel to people where they are. And we need to demonstrate it with love and power.

I do not believe we will reach this increasingly large percentage of people who are closed to church without a demonstration of power and a manifestation of Jesus' love. In a postmodern, pluralistic, syncretistic society, most people are convinced that all deities are the same, that all paths lead to Heaven—if they believe in an afterlife at all. People will not be convinced that Jesus is unique and Lord of all deities unless this truth is demonstrated.

Your claim that Jesus is Lord doesn't prove it to others. They will likely honor your testimony and be happy that it works for you, but most often that will not be enough to convince them that Jesus is Lord of all. In a world where all deities are considered equal, we must demonstrate that Jesus is supreme. It will have to be shown with loving lives of sacrificial service—like that displayed by our Lord—and a supernatural power that brings freedom and fullness to the spiritually oppressed. This is how it was in the first century in cities like Corinth. Paul wrote to that church:

> When I came to you, I did not come with eloquence or human wisdom as I proclaimed to you the testimony about God. For I resolved to know nothing while I was with you except Jesus Christ and him crucified. I came to you in weakness [and] with great fear and trembling. My message and my preaching were not with wise and persuasive words, but with a demonstration of the Spirit's power, so that your faith might not rest on human wisdom, but on God's power (1 Corinthians 2:1-5).

Paul came in weakness. He was authentic, vulnerable, real. He came to serve, not to be served; in this way he was just like Jesus. He came proclaiming Christ: Christ crucified and Christ resurrected. But he also came with a demonstration of the Spirit's power. In the culture we live in today, truth is considered relative, and all deities are considered equal paths to God. How can it be proved that Jesus is Lord of all? How can we show people that Jesus is unique? It is hard to persuade people with arguments when truth is viewed as personal, subjective, and relative. There has to be a demonstration of love and power that is persuasive beyond reason. We proclaim Jesus is King, and we witness to the gospel of the kingdom, but if we want to be effective we must demonstrate that the King has come, that His kingdom is invading the darkness. We must demonstrate the message that this King of Heaven has power to overcome evil and all its effects, just like the early church demonstrated this to its generation. We must operate in the power of God that releases those in bondage, that heals the brokenhearted, that frees people from the power of the enemy.

In a pluralistic, syncretistic society where all deities are considered equal, only the unequal display of Jesus' power will convince people of the supremacy of Christ. If there isn't an unequal display of power, how will people know that Jesus is Lord? If there isn't a tangible display of love, how will they know Jesus is good?

Therefore, if we are going to effectively reach the unreached in this generation, we must help God's people move in power—and that takes authority.

> In a pluralistic, syncretistic society where all deities are considered equal, only the unequal display of Jesus' power will convince people of the supremacy of Christ.

The pathway to release the power of God is the authority that Christ gave us. The early disciples moved in power because Jesus gave them authority (Matthew 10:1f; Luke 10:17f), and they learned how to develop it, walk in it, and use it to overcome evil and its influence on humanity. They demonstrated that Jesus was King, that His kingdom was invading earth. Today we need to learn to operate in authority once again, just like the early church did, so we can reach this generation as they reached theirs.

I grew up in a church where we believed the truths of the gospel, but there was little evidence of God's presence and power. As I read the Gospels and book of Acts, I was convinced that Jesus had not changed and therefore the things the early believers saw could be part of the church today, but I didn't know what to do about it. I was also convinced that the early church advanced rapidly on the heels of God's demonstrative power over the forces of darkness that invaded earth. Then I experienced a fundamental shift: I had a powerful encounter with the Spirit of God when I was in college. It was transformative. I experienced God's presence and power; I now knew it was available. I wanted everyone to experience the reality of Christ, His presence, and His power. So when I began ministry, I preached what I saw in the Scriptures, not my personal lack of experience. For example, I preached that Jesus healed even though, before I started preaching on it, I never saw anyone miraculously healed. In the beginning, I saw very little of what I believed so very much. But I wouldn't give up; I knew there had to be more.

When our experience doesn't match up with what the Bible says, we only have a few options. We can explain away what the Bible plainly teaches to lower it to meet our impotent experience. We may feel better with this approach, but we will live far beneath our potential. We can feel the dissonance between what the Bible says and what we are experiencing, and we can grumble and complain and wait around passively for something to change. Or there is a third option: we can seek to elevate our experience to match what Scripture teaches. I wouldn't let go of what I saw in the Bible—it took time and growth—and eventually I started seeing God's presence and power released in significant ways. It wasn't an easy journey, but I would gladly do it all again.

I am not seeing everything I want to see, but I am seeing far more than I used to see, and it wouldn't have happened without an intentional pursuit to close the gap. The further I got in ministry, the more I fell into a second trap listed above, the one of being discontented. I thought if I just preached faithfully and expected the power of God to be displayed, it would happen easily and quickly and regularly. It didn't. One day I felt the Lord tell me to pursue revival and the things of the kingdom with passion, not to wait passively for their arrival.

So I pursued. And as I pursued, one night the Lord woke me with an audible voice and said, "I am going to teach you about authority." It is the only time the Lord has spoken to me audibly, so I knew this was an important conversation. That night began a new journey in my life. I began to understand that authority is developmental, not just positional. I couldn't wait around passively for God to just show up and make things happen; I had to do my part and develop spiritual authority. And as I began to develop authority, I started to see a new level of demonstration of God's power.

This book will begin to unfold some of the key lessons the Lord taught me about authority that changed my life. I am still learning; I am still growing in spiritual authority. And I am grateful for all the Lord has revealed to me through the Scriptures and His Holy Spirit.

If you want to see a great demonstration of the Lord's presence and power in your life and the lives of those around you so you can advance the kingdom of God to His glory, I pray this book will help you on your journey. May the lessons the Lord has revealed to me benefit you.

One:
The One Irrepressible Need of Our Life: The Presence of God

I used to attend leadership conferences, and rather than leaving with inspiration and ideas, I often left feeling a little depressed. I wasn't sure why, but I knew something was missing. I just didn't know what it was. I was pretty sure it wasn't just me. For all the emphasis on church growth, leadership, and mission that I have heard in my lifetime, according to all the statistics, the church was losing ground. I began to realize that a smaller percentage of people were attending church in the Western world than ever before. I had a simple question: What was wrong?

Something is missing from our leadership model in the church today. If I were to go into most churches and ask about the leadership approach, I would not find much difference between the church leaders and business leaders in that community. For the most part, we employ a business leadership model with a little Jesus thrown on top, a bit like whipped cream added on a sundae. We do the things that business leaders do, we practice the principles they practice, we speak the leadership language they speak; we just add on things like an emphasis on character and prayer. But is this is the leadership model Jesus demonstrated for us, or is there something more that Jesus wants for us?

> For the most part, we employ a business leadership model with a little Jesus thrown on top.

I am not against learning leadership principles from business leaders or *New York Times* best-selling leadership books. I know there is a good deal of overlap between the business world of leadership and the kingdom world of leadership. Actually, I have read hundreds of leadership books in my lifetime. We need to learn wisdom, a biblical category of thought, and learning how to lead effectively is a wisdom category people in leadership positions need. We need to learn how to influence people, cast vision, mobilize volunteers on mission, develop strategy, implement plans, allocate resources, and more. But is this all there is to Jesus' leadership? Is this how Jesus built His church? Was Jesus merely an exceptionally developed leader who was flawless in character and deep in prayer? Or was there something different in His approach to leadership? Is there something fundamentally missing in our leadership model that is out of sync with Jesus' leadership approach?

I've listened to hundreds of leadership teachings and read hundreds of leadership books in an attempt to maximize my effectiveness for advancing Jesus' kingdom. I've gained much from those efforts. It is worthwhile to grow as a leader, but it is also insufficient. Spiritual leadership involves more than human leadership. Jesus led with authority, and that is what set Him apart.

Not only did I read leadership books, I attended the Leadership Summit put on by the Willow Creek Association every year. I attended for the first seventeen years, and usually I took groups of people with me. I learned a lot, grew a lot, and benefited a great deal from the Summits, and again, I am grateful for their influence in my life. But I also felt a certain reality; as I said at the beginning of this chapter, I always left feeling a bit depressed. I would withdraw emotionally partway through the summit. Some of my staff would ask me, "What happens to you when you attend this? You disappear."

> It is worthwhile to grow as a leader, but it is also insufficient. Spiritual leadership involves more than human leadership.

It took me years to figure it out, but I finally got it.

Every time I went I heard people give inspirational talks about vision-casting, strategic thinking, execution of strategy, developing staff, reproducing leaders, mobilizing volunteers, and many other worthy topics. But I would leave feeling depressed because I felt like I didn't have what it takes to fulfill my God-given calling. My assignment from God felt like a mountain that the best of my human efforts could not move. From the time I was a young man I felt God was calling me to fight for renewal—to be part of a movement where the church was free in Christ and full of the Spirit and the Lord was "adding daily" to our lives "those who were being saved," just as it says in the book of Acts. I wanted to fight for renewal in the church, and I wanted to see a great awakening in the country that would change the spiritual landscape of the world.

The question that discomforted my soul was this: "How do you lead a spiritual movement with your best human effort? How do you bring about a spiritual renewal with human leadership only?" There must be something more. A spiritual renewal movement cannot be accomplished with human leadership techniques alone. We cannot produce spiritual results with human ingenuity. We need God. And we cannot simply make our best human plans and just ask God to bless them. We need to be the best leaders we can be, but that alone is not enough, and that alone is not how Jesus modeled kingdom leadership.

The weight of my assignment was mounting on me, and I felt stuck. One day I talked to the Lord about my growing discontent with the state of affairs in the church. I felt the Lord telling me to "preach revival until it comes. You aren't passive about any other area of your life, but you are passively waiting for revival to happen." I realized He was right; I had always waited passively for revival to happen. I expected since it was my calling that if I just went about my business faithfully, God would bring revival; it would just happen. I figured if I preached, called people to live on mission, and prayed faithfully, eventually revival was bound to come. But it didn't, and I felt more and more like a failure, like there was something wrong with me, like I didn't

> I figured if I preached, called people to live on mission, and prayed faithfully, eventually revival was bound to come. But it didn't.

have what it takes. I just wasn't a good enough leader to fulfill God's assignment for me.

Moses Holds the Key

I didn't want to lead a large and successful church; I wanted to be part of a movement of God that impacted our city, region, country, and world. That was what my heart longed for. But it didn't happen, and I was getting discontented. However, a shift started in me the day the Lord spoke to me about preaching revival. That seemed like a good idea, but I didn't understand how to preach revival, and I still felt like I didn't have what it took. I decided to go away to the monastery to meet alone with God; I knew the Lord had to show me something I had been missing. I knew it had to do with authority since He woke me in the night and spoke to me about that very topic. As I waited on the Lord, I sensed the Spirit saying to me, "Study Moses. He holds the key you are looking for." As I obeyed, God reacquainted me with Moses, and I saw things I had never seen before. I started learning about authority. Jesus wasn't just a good leader; Jesus was a man of spiritual authority. And so was Moses.

We read about God's call to Moses in Exodus 3. This was his assignment: to lead a group of people out of a place where the people didn't want them to leave, into a place where the people didn't want them to come, with a group of people who didn't want to take the trip. Welcome to spiritual leadership! This is what it feels like to be a pastor many days! It was a miserable, "God-only-possible" assignment, and Moses felt inadequate for the task. Who could blame him? His first question upon hearing this impossible assignment was, "Who am I?" He felt the weight of the assignment and the inadequacy of his leadership ability. He didn't feel like he had what it took as a leader to accomplish this assignment, and, on top of that, his authority was underdeveloped.

God appeared to Moses in a burning bush. At first, Moses didn't know this was God. He saw a bush on fire that did not burn up, so he went over to check out this amazing sight. God spoke to him out of the bush, revealing Himself to Moses by saying, "I am the God of your fathers, the God of Abraham, the God of Isaac, and the God of Jacob." This is the first time Moses realizes what is happening and to whom he is talking. "At this, Moses hid his face, because he was afraid to look at God." This is the response of someone who carries shame. Shame was blocking Moses from becoming the spiritual leader he needed to be to do the work God was calling him to do.

I teach Soul Care Conferences all over the world, and I call people to come into the light and walk in the light with God and others. I like to use this analogy: Your soul is like a suitcase. I travel a lot, and when I take a trip, I pack nice, neat, clean, folded clothes into my suitcase. By the end of the trip everything is dirty, so I throw all of it in the suitcase and return home. Before I can take my next trip, I have to unpack the suitcase. I have to take out the dirty clothes before I can pack in the nice, neat, clean, folded clothes for my next trip.

Often people are trying to pack the things of God into their lives: freedom, fullness, joy, love, peace, and more godly qualities. But they can't pack those things into the suitcase of their soul because the suitcase is already full. They need to empty the suitcase before they can fill it. Since I call people to unpack the dirty laundry, to bring sin into the light with God, people come to me regularly and say, "I've never told anyone this before." Then they proceed to unpack some secret from the suitcase of their soul. No one ever tells me their secrets and looks

No one ever tells me their secrets and looks me in the eye while doing so; they look down at the floor and stumble over their words.

me in the eye while doing so; they look down at the floor and stumble over their words. That's the power of shame. Shame makes us hide our face. Think about Adam and Eve in the garden: the first thing they did when they rebelled against God was hide. They hid in the garden from God, and they covered up their nakedness. That's shame.

Moses was packing a lot of shame in the suitcase of his soul, and shame always makes you feel inadequate; it makes you feel unworthy. The ultimate question of shame is this: Do I have what it takes? The problem with shame is that it makes things too much about us. Shame produces self-talk filled with self-doubt: "If people really knew me, they wouldn't love me, they wouldn't accept me, they wouldn't follow me. There is something wrong with me. I am broken, damaged, irreparable. I don't have what it takes. Who am I?" Moses had shame because of the murder he committed, striking down and killing an Egyptian in Egypt. He never really dealt with that act; he just ran from it. He had a secret in his soul, and secrets create shame. He relocated to a different area, with different people, and started a different life. But wherever you go, there you are, and you carry your suitcase with you. There is no avoiding it, and whatever you are packing in the suitcase of your soul is impacting you. Moses was packing secrets, and shame was impacting him. Running from your past doesn't keep that past from impacting your present.

Who Am I?

Murder wasn't the beginning of Moses' journey with shame. It started with shame from his family-of-origin issues. Pharaoh set out to kill all the baby boys among the Hebrew slaves because he was afraid the Hebrews were getting too numerous. But Moses' parents sought to save him by shipping him down the river—literally. They put him in a little boat and sent him down the Nile. They did it with pure motives, but when you are a little guy, you can't sort all that out; you just feel rejected and abandoned, unloved and unwanted. Your only way to internalize that event is to once again wonder: *What is wrong with me that even my parents rejected me?* You can't help but feel unloved, unlovable, broken, damaged, and unwanted. This is the beginning of Moses' shame.

Then he was adopted into an Egyptian household, the royal household. But Scripture says the Egyptians wouldn't even eat with Hebrews because that was detestable to them (Genesis 43:32). Moses grew up feeling "less than"; there was prejudice against him. He had significant shame from the rejection and abandonment of his parents, and from the rejection and prejudice he suffered as a former slave boy living in a royal household. Shame is an identity issue that is manifest in community. We often hide when we carry shame because we feel bad about ourselves. We feel that if people really knew us they wouldn't accept us, so we hide from God and others. We build self-protective walls to keep other people from discovering what is in the suitcase of our souls. Many people are so good

> Many people are so good at building walls to hide their shame that they hide it from themselves.

at building walls to hide their shame that they hide it from themselves. They are completely unaware that shame is driving their behavior in life and relationships.

Thus, with all of this shame packed in the suitcase of his soul, when God appears to Moses in the burning bush, and when He first reveals himself to Moses by His name, Moses hides his face (Exodus 3:6). That's shame. Shame makes us afraid to draw near others—especially God. When people struggle with shame, they have intimacy barriers, walls they build to protect themselves from being "found out." If people get too close to us when we carry shame, we feel threatened, fearful, even angry. Sometimes our shame manifests when people get too physically close; we are uncomfortable with close contact. People hug us a little too long and our skin crawls. Other times we feel uncomfortable to get too emotionally close. We share too much about ourselves with a small group of people and we feel violated.

Moses is so fundamentally convinced that he does not have what it takes to fulfill this impossible assignment from God that when God tells him to go to Pharaoh, Moses responds, "Who am I that I should go?" (Exodus 3:11) *Who am I?* He is wrestling with his identity to his core. *Who am I?* I don't have what it takes. *Who am I?* I can't do this. *Who am I?* I am not competent for this assignment. *Who am I?* People won't listen to me; they won't follow me. I can't do this. *Who am I?* This is an assignment beyond my human capacity to lead. *Who am I?* I can't convince Pharaoh to let the people go.

I could relate to Moses; that was exactly how I felt. God had given me an impossible assignment, and I wasn't able to lead people where God was clearly calling me to take them. And no matter how much leadership competency I acquired, I knew the goal was still going to be beyond me. I too had shame packed away in the suitcase of my soul. There were all kinds of reasons for the shame in my suitcase, just like there were many reasons for Moses' shame.

Let me tell one brief story to indicate how shame is formed, and the power it holds. When I was in second grade my brother had a birthday party at the house. All of his class came over; my brother is a year older than me. We had a downstairs bathroom in that house, and the front porch extended out beyond the bathroom window. It was summer, so the window was open. I went to the bathroom during the party, and a kid named Bruce was out on the porch with the rest of my brother's classmates. He looked in the bathroom window, saw me in there, and started mocking me in front of all of the kids. He shamed me. It was such a powerful event in my life that I wouldn't use a public restroom for years. That's the power of shame; it makes us avoid people and hide.

When shame afflicts the soul, the mind works overtime to compensate, to question, to figure it out. Sometimes our minds are tormented with self-doubt. Other times we move toward grandiosity where we compare ourselves with others and imagine ourselves or even fantasize about ourselves in grandiose ways, all the while trying to bolster our identity, which is damaged by shame. We see ourselves in bigger-than-life ways to compensate for our inner sense of inadequacy and shame. Some people resort to power, control, and anger. Others struggle with addiction as they seek to mask the pain of the shame in their souls. Sometimes we just withdraw, feel depressed, and give up. *Who am I?* We feel a need to prove ourselves, and if we

> That's the power of shame; it makes us avoid people and hide.

can't prove ourselves then we feel depressed. Do I have what it takes? It is the fundamental question of a person afflicted with shame. It is the question Moses was immediately drawn to in his conversation with God when faced with his daunting assignment.

One of the things I love about God is that even when we ask the wrong question, God often still gives the right answer. The question Moses asked—*Who am I?*—was the wrong question because he was making it too much about him. Shame always makes it too much about us. Shame is a head-down posture. Put your head down right now. All the way down to your chest. Even if you are in a room full of people, the only person you can see is you, and you have a distorted view of yourself. You don't see all of you when you put your head down; shame never gives an accurate view of ourselves even while making it too much about ourselves at the same time! Shame is an eyes-on-me disease of the soul. Shame forces us to take our eyes off God and put our eyes on ourselves. We may struggle to prove our worth by overachieving, but we are still limited to what we can accomplish, even with all of our best efforts. Shame takes our eyes off God, and it limits our spiritual authority and capacity to move mountains.

The Need for God's Presence

That is one of the fundamental problems of leadership in the church today. We are making it way too much about us: too much about our gifts, our talents, our capabilities, our plans, our programs, our strategies, our resources, and our competencies. Moses struggled in the same way. He was making it too much about him. He asked the wrong question. He shouldn't have asked, "Who am I?" He should have asked,

"Who are you?" Because, if you are going to accomplish the impossible, you need God. Only God has unlimited resources; only God has infinite wisdom; only God has unstoppable power; only God can do the impossible. But God answers Moses with the right answer anyway! He told him, "I will be with you" (Exodus 3:12). This is the key to the impossible. God never gives you an assignment that you can accomplish without Him. When God gives you an assignment, God calls you into partnership. When God calls you into partnership to accomplish the impossible, God promises His presence to get the job done. Only God can do the impossible; the key to accomplishing the impossible is the presence of God. This is the key that begins to unlock a different leadership that is more biblical, less businesslike, more God-centered, less me-centered, more about His authority, and less about our human ability to make something happen. We need God's presence to accomplish God's assignment. When you have a God-only-possible assignment, the one indispensable need of your life is the presence of God.

Have you ever noticed that at beginning of both of the great redemptive movements of God, He appears as a fire that doesn't consume anything? Here in the Moses story, God appears in a burning bush, but the bush does not get consumed. In the book of Acts when the Spirit is poured out on Pentecost, God appears as tongues of fire, but nothing is consumed. Why does God appear as a fire that consumes nothing? It is at least in part because He is showing us that He doesn't need any fuel. He is the God who is self-sufficient, self-sustaining. All the rest of us have needs, but not God. We need Him. We need God's presence to accomplish God's kingdom assignments.

It is the presence of God that changes us. It is the presence of God that empowers us. It is the presence of God that enables us to change the spiritual atmosphere over a family, a church, a town, a city, a region. It is the presence of God that makes all the difference that we cannot make on our own, even with all of our best efforts. *The one irrepressible need of our life is the presence of God.* "I will be with you." In essence, God is saying to Moses: "I know you feel inadequate. I know you feel like you don't have what it takes to accomplish this impossible assignment. But I will be with you. And that is enough." The one irrepressible need of our life is the presence of God.

> The one irrepressible need of our life is the presence of God.

What I love about Moses is that he so internalizes this lesson that for the rest of his life his number one priority is the pursuit of the presence of God. He discovers that the one irrepressible need of his life is the presence of God, and nothing will keep him from pressing in and pressing through to the presence. In Exodus 19 the Lord calls Moses up to Mount Sinai to give him the Ten Commandments. The scene is terrifying. "On the morning of the third day there was thunder and lightning, with a thick cloud over the mountain, and a very loud trumpet blast. Everyone in the camp trembled. Then Moses led the people out of the camp to meet with God and they stood at the foot of the mountain. Mount Sinai was covered with smoke, because the Lord descended on it in fire.

The smoke billowed up from it like smoke from a furnace, and the whole mountain trembled violently. . . . The Lord descended to the top of Mount Sinai and called Moses to the top of the mountain. So Moses went up" (Exodus 19:16-20). We used to sing a song about this scene. It went something like this: "Like Moses we enter the cloud, we aren't afraid, we aren't afraid." I love the song and the sentiment. But I read this scene and I think: Wait a minute. That isn't true. As a matter of fact, Hebrews tells us Moses was trembling with fear (Hebrews 12:21). This old man was trembling in terror; his knees were knocking under his toga. He was scared witless. But he went up anyway. Why? Because he learned the one irrepressible need of his life was the presence of God. He was willing to pay any price to get there, and there is always a price for the presence of God. When it becomes less about us and more about God, we discover that we must pay the price to enter His presence and carry His presence.

Moses stayed on the mountaintop with God forty days and forty nights. Can you imagine this? At the end of their time together, a bad scene emerges. It is the golden calf incident; this is not Aaron's finest hour. After this, the Lord makes Moses an offer: How about if I start over with you? We will wipe these people out and start over with you. Exodus 32:9, 10: "'I have seen these people,' the Lord said to Moses, 'and they are a stiff-necked people. Now leave me alone so that my anger may burn against them and that I may destroy them. Then I will make you into a great nation.'" That is never an offer God has made to me as a pastor! I think there were days He might have been afraid I would take Him up on it. But Moses sought the favor of God for the people; he pleaded for the people to be saved for the sake of God's own reputation. And the Lord relented.

Listen, I'll let you in on a little secret. God never intended on blowing up the people. He was testing what was in the heart of His servant Moses, and what He discovered was that Moses had hung out in the Master's presence for so long to this point that the things on the heart of the Master were now on the heart of the servant. He was being transformed by the presence of God. The things that were on the heart of the Father had now taken root in the heart of His son. Not only that, but in the beginning when faced with a terrifying calling, Moses, full of shame, asks, "Who am I?" He makes it all about him. But now Moses knows it is all about God, and God's reputation, and God's glory. Shame produces self-focus, making it too much about us. The presence and grace of God cure the heart of shame and break us free from self-focus. The presence of God is transformational. This time Moses asks, "What will people think about you? What will the nations say?" (Exodus 32:11-14) "Why should the Egyptians say, 'It was with evil intent that he brought them out, to kill them in the mountains and to wipe them off the face of the earth'? Turn from your fierce anger; relent and do not bring disaster on your people. Remember your servants Abraham, Isaac, and Israel, to whom you swore by your own self: 'I will make your descendants as numerous as the stars in the sky and I will give your descendants all this land I promised them, and it will be their inheritance forever.' Then the Lord relented and did not bring on his people the disaster he had threatened."

Then the Lord, in so many words, tells Moses, "All right. I won't blow them up. But I'm not going with you. I'll send an angel" (see Exodus 33:2, 3). But Moses won't relent. He has learned his lesson: the one irrepressible need of his life is the presence of God. You can't do the impossible without the presence going before you, with you, in you. So he pleads:

"Remember that this nation is your people." *The only thing that marks us as the people of God is the presence of God.* It isn't going to church, it isn't reading our Bible, it isn't praying. It isn't being good, trying harder, or accomplishing great things for God. It is the presence of God, and Moses has learned this lesson. The Lord promises to go with them—"My Presence will go with you"—which is really what God had wanted all along.

But Moses isn't done here. He is gaining boldness as he is unpacking shame, and Moses presses in for even more in the thirty-third chapter of Exodus: He asks God to show him his glory. This would be an irreverent request if it came from a mere acquaintance, but this is the shamelessly audacious request of a rare but true friend of God.

> This would be an irreverent request if it came from a mere acquaintance, but this is the shamelessly audacious request of a rare but true friend of God.

And, amazingly, God grants his request.

Face to Face

In the midst of this scene a phrase emerges that is a vital understanding to this man's enormous spiritual leadership and authority: "The Lord would speak to Moses face to face, as one speaks to a friend" (Exodus 33:11). This is the man who hid his face from God at his first God-sighting, but now he has become a face-to-face friend of God. He has learned that he needs God above all things, and he is pressing in and pressing through to that one end.

The story goes on with Moses experiencing victories and setbacks, highs and lows. There are leadership betrayals and failures of the people and some of Moses' own failures mixed into the chaos. The worst of them all occurs when his brother and sister rebel against him (Numbers 12). It is one thing to suffer a leadership betrayal from people under you, but when it is from your own family, that cuts to the heart. Aaron and Miriam, his own brother and sister, rebel against him. They say, "Who do you think you are? God doesn't only speak to you. He speaks to us as well." Right in the middle of this family dispute a phenomenal event occurs—and for the only time in the history of the Bible. God descends to earth to defend a man. There are times God defends someone in Heaven (as with Job), but this time God descends to earth to defend His friend Moses. The Lord says in his defense, "When there are prophets of the Lord among you, I reveal myself to them in visions, I speak to them in dreams. But this is not true of my servant Moses; he is faithful in all my house. With him I speak face to face" (Numbers 12:6-8). God is saying: He is faithful in all my house; he is my one true, faithful friend.

Imagine! Could there be a more noble goal in all the universe than to become a true and faithful friend to God? Most translations render the last phrase I quoted as "With him I speak face to face," and the TNIV is among them. But the actual Hebrew words have shifted. It is no longer "face to face"; it is literally "with him I speak mouth to mouth." Moses has moved from a man who hid his face from God to a man who was a face-to-face friend with God to a man who was a mouth-to-mouth lover of God. No wonder his words carry such weight in Heaven!

A Hand Upon the Throne

There is a famous scene in Moses' life in Exodus 17. It is the scene in which Joshua is leading the Israelites into battle against the Amalekites. While Joshua is fighting in the valley below, Moses climbs to the top of a hill. "As long as Moses held up his hands, the Israelites were winning, but whenever he lowered his hands, the Amalekites were winning" (Exodus 17:11). I always picture the human realities to the biblical stories. I don't think Moses noticed exactly what was taking place right away. That's just human nature. I suspect that the old man climbs the hill, and when he reaches its peak he sees his people being overwhelmed, and he starts praying. He gets into it; he is praying with all his heart. He is on his feet, he lifts his hands with his staff of authority, and he calls out to his God. With this, he notices that the tide of the battle has begun to change.

But he is an old man and he gets tired, so he sits down for a rest. While Moses is sitting the battle shifts again and the Israelites are being whipped, and his concerns energize him once again to pray, to plead for victory. As he stands and lifts his hands with his rod of authority over his head, sure enough —the tide turns again. I think this likely happens a few times and finally Aaron or Hur notice this and say to him, "Hey, Mo, every time you stand and lift your hands we are winning, but when you rest your hands, we start to lose. You sit down on that rock over there, and we will lift up your hands over your head as you plead for the victory." And the victory came. The Amalekites were focused on Joshua and the army; they had no idea the real battle was being fought in the heavenlies on a hill by an old man in a toga. If the Amalekite leaders understood that, they would have just tried to kill the old man on

The Amalekites were focused on Joshua and the army; they had no idea the real battle was being fought in the heavenlies on a hill by an old man in a toga.

the hill. But, like them, we often focus our attention on the earthly battles and get distracted from spiritual leadership assignments necessary for victory. At the end of the battle Moses writes down a key phrase to summarize what happened. The ESV translates the phrase this way: "A hand upon the throne of the Lord" (Exodus 17:16).

A hand upon the throne of the Lord. This is spiritual leadership. It isn't about human capability, human resources, human ingenuity, or our best human effort. This is spiritual authority. *Spiritual authority is the capacity to touch Heaven and change the outcomes of earth.* It is the capacity to invite the presence of God to intervene and move our mountains. This isn't mere human vision, strategy, or good execution. All of those things are necessary, but in the end they can only produce what humans can produce with their best effort. If we are going to see the things only God can do, then we need to be spiritual leaders who exercise spiritual authority. We need to attend to His presence; our lives must be characterized by His presence, saturated with His presence. We must develop a face-to-face intimacy with God that allows us to touch Heaven and change earth. We need to press so deeply into His presence that we carry His presence and bring the weight of His presence to bear upon our present problems and bring God's victory to our impossibilities. We need to learn the lesson of Moses: that the one irrepressible need of our life is the presence of God, a hand upon the throne. We must learn to touch Heaven and change the outcomes of earth. We must learn to be deeply intimate friends of God who exercise spiritual authority to change earthly outcomes.

We have focused on leadership for a long time now in the church, and yet we continue to see the statistics that fewer people are attending church than ever before in the West, and this in spite of all our best leadership efforts. Spiritual movements aren't birthed with mere human effort; spiritual movements are birthed when the presence of God comes and shifts something in the atmosphere of the heavenly realms. Spiritual movements are birthed when a spiritual leader encounters the presence of God, is marked by the power of God, and learns to touch Heaven and change the outcomes on earth. If we do what we can do, we will accomplish what we can with our human ability. If we press into His presence, touch Heaven, and change the spiritual atmosphere on earth, we can see what God can fully do. This is spiritual authority.

Spiritual authority is the ability to contend with the heavenly realities through spiritual leadership, and this affects the outcomes of the earthly realms and manifests the Kingdom of God in our midst. Spiritual authority gives us the ability to dismantle hell wherever we go. This, too often, is missing in the church. This is what I was missing in my life. I was trying to lead a spiritual movement with human leadership and human effort, and I constantly felt I didn't have what it takes. That was because I didn't. I have what it takes to lead what my gifting allows me to influence, but I can't move mountains. I can speak effectively, but I can't change human hearts. I can pray for the sick, but I can't heal human bodies. I can talk about the inviolable principles of the soul, but I cannot free one shackled soul. I was making it too much about me, just like Moses at the beginning: "Who am I?" I was asking the wrong question, and I was left with this disquieting sense of my own inadequacy and the inevitable lid of the limitation of my resulting self-focus. I could not move the mountains before me. They stood in front of me mocking my human limitations; they stood as a monument to my human frailties. The mountains also stand as invitations to recognize the one irrepressible need of my life. The day that I closely studied the life of Moses, something inside of me shifted permanently. I realized what that one irrepressible need of my life was. I didn't merely need more knowledge or more skills, I needed to seek God's face and expand my capacity to carry His presence.

Don't get me wrong. It wasn't like I didn't pray before I had this encounter with God through Moses' life. I prayed; I spent time with God nearly every day. I prayed before we made plans seeking God's wisdom, and I prayed after we made plans. John 15 had motivated much of my approach and philosophy of ministry. Jesus says, "I am the vine; you are the branches. If you remain in me and I in you, you will bear much fruit; apart from me you can do nothing" (John 15:5). I believed that. I believed I could not produce lasting spiritual fruit without abiding in Jesus. I sought God for His anointing, His power, His help, His wisdom, His provision. But I also spent most of my early days of ministry seeking God's hands, not His face.

> I sought God for His anointing, His power, His help, His wisdom, His provision. But I also spent most of my early days of ministry seeking God's hands, not His face.

The Moses story isn't a story of prayer; it is a story of intimacy. It isn't a story about seeking God's hands; it is a story about seeking

God's face. It isn't a story about maximizing human capacity; it's a story about carrying the presence of God to confront our impossibilities. I prayed, but not often enough like that. I sought His help, not His presence. I pursued His intervention, not intimacy with Him. I pursued God for results because I really believed I couldn't do anything apart from Him. But spiritual authority is birthed in intimacy with God, not in pursuit of God's power.

Moses didn't pursue God's hands alone; he pursued God's face. He moved from a man who hid his face to a man who pursued God's face to a man who became face-to-face friends with God to a man who became a mouth-to-mouth lover with the God of the impossible. This is what enabled Moses to touch Heaven and change earth; this intimacy was the key to his authority, and this empowered him to be used by God to move mountains. When I got that lesson that day, I realized I needed to make the pursuit of the presence of God my number one priority. Not ministry. Not fruit. Not power. Not help. Not wisdom. Not answers to prayer. Not His hands. His face. I need God. The one irrepressible need of my life is for the presence of God. Only then can I become a man of spiritual authority. If I am ever going to break out of the prison of my human limitations, His presence is the key. If I am ever going to lay a hand upon the throne, if I am going to touch Heaven and change the outcomes on earth, I must become a face-to-face friend with God. This is the ground upon which spiritual authority emerges.

And like Moses, for many of us the thing that prevents us from this level of intimacy with God is the stuff we are carrying around in the suitcase of our souls. Things like shame. It was in my suitcase still, as it was in Moses' suitcase. It is most

> It is most frequently our soul issues that keep us from our next level of intimacy with God.

frequently our soul issues that keep us from our next level of intimacy with God.

Authority Versus Authoritarian

Before I close this chapter, there is one matter I must address. We have to discuss the concept of authority because authority has a negative connotation for many people today. We live in an anti-authoritarian society in the United States. We were a country founded in rebellion. We have deep-rooted and long-held suspicions against people in positions of authority. That attitude has only grown since the 1960s. It has been further aggravated by some of the underpinnings of postmodernism. All worldviews are broken. I am not here to tear down a postmodern perspective, but like modernism and every other perspective in a sin-stained planet, it is a flawed worldview.

Postmodernism holds the philosophical belief that if there is truth, it is difficult—perhaps even impossible—to identify clearly and with any certainty. Therefore, in layman's terms, you can't know the truth with certainty, so everyone gets to define their own version of truth. The one thing that is left as an absolute is that you absolutely have no right to tell anyone that they are wrong about their choices. The one value that has risen to the top of all values in this societal worldview is the value of "tolerance." One problem with this outcome is that we have badly defined this word. We have essentially assumed that tolerance means everyone is entitled to their opinion, and all opinions are equally valid. That's not tolerance; that's just crazy. If this were true, Hitler's viewpoints would be equal to those of Mother Teresa.

As a result of this philosophical shift we hold that anyone has a right to self-define, and that if you disagree with an individual's self-definition, you are an intolerant, bigoted, judgmental, hateful person. Therefore, I must agree with your opinion. However, if acceptance equals agreement, then diversity is a myth. We have held to the preeminence of tolerance precisely because we have wanted to be diverse, but our wrong working definition of tolerance is threatening the diversity we honor. If I must agree with you in order to accept you, then we cannot have diversity; we only have uniformity. Acceptance does not mean that we agree with everyone else.

> Acceptance means that I respect you and your opinions, and I value you and honor you and treat you with dignity and respect. I honor your freedom and choices.

Tolerance, true tolerance, should never demand agreement or uniformity. Tolerance means that I honor your opinions and treat you with dignity and respect. I allow you to make your choices without trying to shame you or bully you into changing. I honor your free will, and I treat you with dignity as I let you decide your way in life. But with our intense focus on tolerance, we have actually become less tolerant, and more shaming; we have become less accepting and more judgmental; we have become less unified and more polarized; we have become less peace-loving and more angry as a culture. Diversity cannot thrive in this atmosphere of misunderstood tolerance. Acceptance means that I respect you and your opinions, and I value you and honor you and treat you with dignity and respect. I honor your freedom and choices, but I don't have to agree with you in order to accept you.

The by-product of this system of belief is that anyone who takes a stand on a moral issue is suspect. They are seen as authoritarian. But Jesus took many stands. He was not a wishy-washy preacher who changed His opinions when the latest opinion polls were tallied. Yet Jesus valued people over opinions; He honored love above all things. Jesus was able to hang around at parties with prostitutes, and they did not feel judged because He simply loved them. He wasn't unclear about His position on sexual values, but He never wavered on His unrelenting commitment to love people. Jesus had spiritual authority but was never guilty of authoritarianism. Authoritarianism shifts into control and abuse of power; it is coercive. Spiritual authority is not that at all. True spiritual authority is not about strong opinions; it is about the ancient weighty wisdom of God cloaked in His presence and marked by His love. Spiritual authority gives a weightiness to our words, not because we are wise or angry, but because we carry His presence.

People said Jesus spoke as one who has authority and not as one of the teachers of the day. Exercising true spiritual authority is not an abuse of power. It is not about being dogmatic or opinionated. It is not about shouting down your opponent or dishonoring or disrespecting someone's viewpoints. It is not ever about shaming or controlling. True spiritual authority is a biblical concept. It flows from humility, not arrogance. It thrives in an atmosphere of grace, not judgment. It is contending against the spiritual powers and authorities in the heavenly realms. It is not a battle with people—they are not the enemy; people are to be loved. It is established in intimacy, not in an angry conveyance of truth.

Our words carry a weightiness not because of the power of our arguments, but because of the power of God's presence in our lives. His presence gives our words an unusual weightiness. Our proclamations and actions ring true not because of our forcefulness, but because they flow from God's eternal kingdom truths embedded in God's enormous heart of grace. True spiritual authority flows out of a deep, intimate relationship with God that produces authentic revelation, and through the intimacy and revelation we carry His presence. People of authentic spiritual authority carry an unmistakable gravitas that comes without control or reliance on human forcefulness. True spiritual leaders who carry authentic spiritual authority are the most magnanimous people in the room. When we forfeit magnanimity, we forgo spiritual authority.

When we fail to operate out of the grace that allows for authority, we tend to operate out of power and control. We use the force of our opinions to win the day and control events and people. We shame people with forceful demands to control behavior. Rather than our words carrying the weightiness of His presence and revelation, we weigh people down with the force of our opinions, demands, and words. This type of leadership is not biblical, and it is not indicative of true authority. It is the leadership of the Gentile leaders, who Jesus said "lord it over" others (Matthew 20:25)—it is not the leadership of Jesus. It is the voice of religion, legalism, fear, shame, and control.

In this book I want to take a look at true spiritual authority. It is both positional and developmental. We will look at where it comes from, how to exercise it in authentic ways, and how to develop it. I want to expand upon one line I think is critical to developing spiritual authority.

Spiritual authority is rooted in identity,
expanded in intimacy, and activated by faith.

This was true in Moses' life. When he was fueled by shame (an identity issue), he misused power and committed murder, and then he ran and hid. Only in the presence of God did his identity get healed and rooted deeply. Only then was he able to make it less about him and more about God. This grace that cured his shame also enabled him to become the intimate friend of God. His newfound security enabled him to draw so near to God that he could lay a hand upon the throne. His security in God's love and his intimate friendship with God deepened his faith and empowered him to take faith-filled risks. It is not always true that the more we know about God, the more we trust God. But it is always true that the more we draw near to God in intimacy, the deeper our trust will grow. Moses believed God for the impossible and saw it come about. Together, as identity, intimacy, and faith were developed in Moses, his authority expanded and he touched Heaven and changed earth.

This book will build upon this statement: *Spiritual authority is rooted in identity, expanded in intimacy, and activated by faith.* Spiritual authority has changed my leadership. I am still growing in it, both in my understanding and in my practice. I am utterly convinced that spiritual authority is essential to true spiritual leadership. It was the leadership model that Jesus used and empowered His disciples to use. Let's explore it together and learn to lead with spiritual leadership and spiritual authority for the sake of God's Kingdom mission in the world today.

Two:
Learning About
Authority

Moses' story really spoke to me. I felt called to fight for revival, but I knew I couldn't make that happen with mere human capacity and my best leadership efforts. It was a God-only-possible assignment that required more than the business leadership model could accomplish. I needed to develop spiritual authority if I was going to fulfill God's call to fight for renewal. I could develop leaders, mobilize people on mission, and teach effective principles for life change—and, likely, if I did all of that effectively, the church would grow. In fact, the church did grow; we grew to about seven hundred people in New England. But overall, fewer people were attending church in our region than ever before.

We were seeing life change, but we were losing the battle for the region. My calling was for revival, not simply to grow a church. My best leadership efforts were not sufficient to see revival come. Good leadership competencies are necessary;

they are important. But I came to realize that without the development of spiritual authority they are not enough to accomplish what only God can accomplish.

We could grow a church, but we couldn't change the spiritual atmosphere of a region. We could run effective programs, but we couldn't cast out demons, heal the sick, or change a condition of the human heart without authority. I had to learn how to touch Heaven to change earth; I needed to move in spiritual authority.

Moving mountains is more about authority than human leadership, competency, or capacity.

The Disciples Learn About Authority

The disciples were in the same boat. They too had to learn about authority; they couldn't bring about a demonstration of the kingdom without it.

One day Jesus was on the Mount of Transfiguration with Pete, Jim, and John—yep, the big three. The rest of the disciples were down below, and they were trying to cast a demon out of a young boy. The boy was terrorized; he often had seizures that caused him to fall into fire or water. The demons were trying to take his life. The father brought the boy to Jesus' disciples hoping to get him free, to heal him and make him whole; he was hoping to bring an end to this torment. He had surely heard of the ministry of Jesus. He probably knew people who were transformed by Jesus' touch and teaching. He came hopeful; he came expecting a miracle. Any parent who has ever had a child in jeopardy knows the desperation of this father. Desperation is often the platform of breakthrough because it makes us humble enough to be open to new solutions; desperation is often the birthplace of faith because dire cir-

> Desperation is often the platform of breakthrough because it makes us humble enough to be open to new solutions.

cumstances cause us to cry out to God for the breakthrough we need. This father came with his boy in hopeful expectation. But Jesus wasn't there, and the disciples couldn't help despite their best efforts. The demon would not leave. It was a devastating moment for this father; it made his faith wobble.

Fortunately for him, Jesus came down from the mountain before the father and his son left for home. The man approached Jesus and knelt before him. Desperate. Pleading. "'Lord, have mercy on my son,' he said. 'He has seizures and is suffering greatly. He often falls into the fire or into the water. I brought him to your disciples, but they could not heal him'" (Matthew 17:15, 16). Jesus addresses the disciples first, and in what sounds like a bit of exasperation. "'You unbelieving and perverse generation,' Jesus replied. 'How long shall I stay with you? How long shall I put up with you? Bring the boy here to me'" (Matthew 17:17).

It's extremely important to note that Jesus expected them to be able to cast out this demon. He expects them to heal the boy. He expects them to be further along by this point. It is, in fact, utterly essential to His eternal plan that they learn to move in authority as He did. It is essential because He is going to return to His Father, and He is planning on leaving the advancement of His kingdom in their hands. They must get this. It isn't optional. If they don't get it, they will be left merely with what only humans can accomplish, and that isn't what the kingdom of God is about. The kingdom of God is about the disruption of hell and the destruction of the devil's works.

If they didn't get this, they would only see human normal, not kingdom normal. Kingdom normal comes with a demonstration of supernatural power that is unmistakably linked to the supremacy of Jesus. The proclamation of the kingdom must be authenticated with a demonstration of power, and there can be no power without authority. It is essential to the establishment of the kingdom that they learn this lesson.

Jesus rebukes them for their unbelief, and He even goes so far as to call them perverse! The Greek word here for perverse is a word that means to distort. They were distorting the gospel of the kingdom by their lack of understanding of authority and their inability to demonstrate power to heal this boy. They were distorting the gospel of the kingdom because this was not the message Jesus proclaimed. Jesus proclaimed the in-breaking of the kingdom, the dismantling of hell, the invasion of Heaven's victories on hell's turf. To proclaim a kingdom devoid of the power of the King is a perversion of the message. This is a tough day for the nine disciples. I think old Pete, Jim, and John were glad they missed out on this one.

Jesus rebukes the demon, it comes out of the boy, and the boy is healed from that moment. Afterward, when the disciples are alone with Jesus, they ask Him the ultimate question: "Why couldn't we drive it out?" It's coaching time. They have done this before. Jesus had sent them out (Matthew 10) to cast out demons, heal the sick, and preach the gospel of the kingdom. We know they had success at that time because Luke records that when he sent out the seventy-two to do the same, they came back and reported that "even the demons submit to us in your name" (Luke 10:17).

So on this particular day, the disciples' real question is: "Lord, we've done this before, and we know how to do this.

We've seen it work in the past. What went wrong this time? Why couldn't we cast this one out?"

Authority and Intimacy

Many of you probably recall Jesus' answer, this one from Mark's gospel: "This kind can come out only by prayer" (Mark 9:29). Some translations add "and fasting." Most people simply assume Jesus was teaching that some kinds of demons cannot be cast out except by prayer and fasting. But that is not what He was teaching. I know that is not what He was teaching for at least two reasons. First, Jesus casts the demon out immediately, and He didn't pray or fast as He commanded it to leave. He doesn't need to pray or fast to cast out this demon. He simply commands the demon to leave and it leaves. Second, Jesus had already taught them how demons are cast out; they are driven out by authority (Matthew 10:1f). This is an authority problem. This is not a kingdom problem that can be resolved with great programming, outstanding leadership competencies, or mere human confidence. This is a kingdom problem that can only be resolved with spiritual authority, and the disciples find themselves lacking just that, and it distorts the message they proclaim.

Jesus taught them this principle when he sent them out the first time. Matthew 10:1 records, "Jesus called his twelve disciples to him and gave them authority to drive out evil spirits and to heal every disease and sickness." He gave them authority to cast out demons and heal the sick. In Luke's version the words are shifted slightly. Luke writes, "When Jesus had called the Twelve together, he gave them power and authority to drive out all demons and cure diseases, and he sent them out to proclaim the kingdom of God and to heal the sick" (Luke

9:1). Matthew says he gave them authority to heal "*every* disease." And Luke says he gave them authority to drive out "all demons." So, between Matthew and Luke we see that we have authority to drive out *all* demons and cure all diseases. But the key in both passages is authority. If we are going to see the things of the kingdom, if we are going to have a demonstration of the gospel of the kingdom, then we must learn how to understand, utilize, and develop spiritual authority.

Authority and Faith

In Matthew's gospel, he records a different answer to the disciples' question, "Why couldn't we cast it out?" The gospels do not contradict each other; rather, taken together they portray a more complete version of the conversation Jesus had with His friends. In Matthew 17:20, 21, Jesus answered, "Because you have so little faith. Truly I tell you, if you have faith as small as a mustard seed, you can say to this mountain, 'Move from here to there,' and it will move. Nothing will be impossible for you."

I think the more complete version of the conversation went something like this: Disciples: "Why couldn't we drive it out? We've done this before." Jesus: "On a scale of one to ten, this one was a 'five.' You've driven out the 'fours,' but this one was stronger. You have developed enough authority to drive out the fours, but if you are going to develop the authority to drive out the more powerful spirits, you are going to have to pray and fast. This will increase your intimacy with the Father. And as you draw near to the Father and me, you will have more faith. You will develop more trust that the bigger ones will leave in my name too. As you pray and fast and increase your faith, you will develop your spiritual authority, which is the key to driving out demons."

Jesus didn't need to pray and fast because His authority was plenty large enough to cast out this demon. His instruction is for them, and He is teaching them how to develop authority. He has already told them that the key to healing the sick and driving out demons is authority. But authority isn't static, it's dynamic. It must be developed.

Developing Our Potential

I don't believe everyone has the same amount of potential authority. Jesus told the parable of the talents, which has clear meaning; some people are given one talent, some two, and some five (Matthew 25:14-30). Some people would claim that God isn't being fair, but God isn't unfair because we are only judged according to what we are given. The guy with two talents doubled his total and received the same commendation as the guy with five talents who doubled his total. They are given different amounts but only judged according to what they have been given. That is fair treatment.

> Jesus will give you what you need to get the job done, but the path to accomplish it will be different. Don't compare yourself with others; just be faithful to develop what God has given you.

The reality is not everyone gets the same abilities in life. Suppose you are given the spiritual gift of helps as your dominant spiritual gift, and on a scale of one to ten your gift is a 'five'; someone else is given an apostolic gift that has the potential for a 'ten.' The person with the "ten" apostolic gifting is always going to have more authority potential. But regardless of what potential authority we've been given, we need to develop our authority to reach our potential. By the way, this doesn't mean that the person with the "five" helps gift can't drive out tough demons, but that person likely will have to pray and fast more, team up with others, and it will take longer. Jesus will give you what you need to get the job done, but the path to accomplish it will be different. Don't compare yourself with others; just be faithful to develop what God has given you.

Most people who teach on spiritual authority—which, sadly, isn't taught very often in the evangelical church—teach that it is positional. If we just understand who we are in Christ, then we can pray and command and make things happen. And while spiritual authority is positional, it isn't only positional; it is also developmental. Our position or our identity in Christ is vital to understand, and we will look at that shortly. But it is also equally important to understand that spiritual authority must be developed, and therefore we must understand how it is developed if we are ever going to reach our potential as Christ followers. Just like the disciples, there are mountains in our lives right now that we cannot move until we expand our level of spiritual authority. We must grow and develop our authority just like we must grow and develop our intimacy with God, moving further into maturity in Christlikeness.

I have a gift in preaching, but that gift isn't static. It is dynamic. I've had to grow and develop this gift the Lord gave me. It was in me, but I still had to develop it to reach my current level as a preacher, and I will have to continue to grow to reach the next level. God has given many people a gift in preaching, but not all preachers have the same potential; not all are given the same level of gifting. All of us are required to faithfully steward the gift we have been given and develop it to our full potential. God gave me the gift, but I had responsibility to nurture the gift, to grow it to its full potential. I am not responsible for any other preacher's gift; I am responsible for the growth, development, and stewardship of the gift God has entrusted to me.

Paul told Timothy, "For this reason I remind you to fan into flame the gift of God, which is in you through the laying on of my hands" (2 Timothy 1:6). Paul exercised authority and imparted a spiritual gift to Timothy, and then he exhorted him to fan it into flame, to develop it to its full potential. I had to develop the spiritual gift given to me, so I went on to get a doctorate degree in preaching, I read thousands of pages on preaching and communication, and I have spent thousands of hours communicating and learning how to preach and communicate more effectively. This is the way the spiritual life works. This is one of the reasons Jesus uses so many agricultural illustrations to indicate the way growth works in the spiritual realm. It is much like the world of plants; there should be development, maturity, growth, and reproduction. Someone needs to cultivate the plants to their full potential. The farmer needs to sow the seed, water, weed, and cultivate the garden. We too should see progress in our spiritual development, but it doesn't come without intentional effort. Healthy things grow. When we are spiritually healthy, we are growing in intimacy with God, in maturity, in the exercise of our gifts and abilities, in our capacity to love others, and in our spiritual authority.

I started doing deliverance ministry, casting out demonic spirits, when I was twenty-five. I had no experience and little training. I had taken a class on deliverance called Power Encounter (I now teach this class as a professor), but I had never seen it done successfully. I had seen one deliverance modeled, but no demons were cast out because the person would not repent and the demons did not have to leave. Deliverance wasn't ever talked about in my church growing up. I didn't have any worldview for deliverance. Unfortunately, our Western worldview often distorts our biblical lenses. I got into ministry as an assistant pastor of a traditional church that, like my home church, had no experience or worldview for deliverance. So the first month on the job someone came into my office who was afflicted with depression, anxiety, and panic attacks. I asked her to tell me her story. Your story is linked with your symptoms. Tell me your symptoms and I can probably guess your story. Tell me your story, and I'll know what you're wrestling with most of the time. We cannot live life divorced from our story.

When I asked this woman her story, she told me her mother was a voodoo priestess and that she herself had been a voodoo practitioner. She was hearing voices; the voices were blasphemous and telling her to hurt herself. I didn't have any experience, but this seemed clearly dark to me. So I took a risk. I asked, "Have you ever considered that your problem could be spiritual in nature?" She said, "You think I have demons, don't you?" I said, "Yes, I do." She replied, "I know I do. I hear their voices. I know what they sound like. I worshiped them." And so I dove into my first deliverance. I had no idea what I was doing, but I was convinced Jesus didn't want her to live with these tormenting spirits and that God was with me. Understand: I didn't get a junior Holy Spirit; I got the same Holy Spirit that was in Jesus. And with the help of God, and the promptings of the Holy Spirit, I got her free from those tormenting spirits.

Since that day I've literally done thousands of deliverances because I lead Soul Care Conferences all over the world in which I train people on the principles of freedom shown in my book, and I help people get free from demonization.

I have developed authority by getting in over my head on a regular basis.

Accessing the Keys to the Kingdom

When I started in deliverance ministry, I often got stuck, just like the disciples. There were times I had no idea what to do. There were times I couldn't get the spirits to give up their names or other information I needed. I went as far as I could with the knowledge and wisdom and authority I had. When I hit a wall, I said to the person, "I don't know what to do. We've been at this for over two hours, and you are tired, and I am tired, and I'm not sure what to do next. But don't worry. Jesus knows what to do, and He will show us. Let's take a break for a few days and pray and fast. If you're willing to pray and fast for your freedom, I will pray and fast too. We can come back next week and meet again. I promise you two things: first, the Lord wants to get you free. He doesn't want anyone to have demons. Second, I will stay with you as long as you are willing, and I will pray and fast with you and fight for your freedom."

> When I started in deliverance ministry, I often got stuck, just like the disciples. There were times I had no idea what to do.

As pastor of a local church, I often had to do multiple sessions with my people to get them free, but as we prayed and fasted and waited on the Lord, He would give us the wisdom we needed and, in the end, the person would be set free.

Here is an important truth: Once I prayed and fasted for that particular demonic situation and the Lord gave me the key to unlock that shackle, I never needed to pray and fast over that one again. The next time I ran into that demonic situation, I knew what to do. I had that key to the kingdom on my key ring, so to speak, and I knew how to use it. When I ran into the same type of demon again, I took that key out, unlocked the shackle, and moved right through that deliverance because I had developed authority. This is what Jesus meant by "this kind comes out only by prayer and fasting" (Mark 9:29).

I'll give you a concrete example from the realm of deliverance ministries. When a person has been sexually abused, most of the time the person will be afflicted with demonic spirits because spirits prey on those who have been victimized in this way. Sadly, many times the person is tormented by these terrible beings. Sometimes, for example, the demon will give them sexual images while they are in worship or reading their Bible or in prayer. They are trying desperately to follow Jesus, and yet they get these disturbing images. They often feel this is their fault; they feel like a pervert. But the truth is, this isn't their fault; they have demons that came in when they were abused (or were inherited from a parent who was abused), and they need deliverance. The demon gives them the sexual images, and then he condemns them for having the thoughts. It's vicious.

The problem is that sexual spirits are particularly tricky.

> The problem is that sexual spirits are particularly tricky. They hide extremely well. They have blocking spirits.

They hide extremely well. They have blocking spirits, and the blocking spirit's entire function is to keep the sexual spirits from being discovered. So even when people who have some experience in deliverance try to do the deliverance, they often do not get victims of sexual abuse free from these sexual spirits. They will get some other spirits out, but the sexual abuse spirits will remain hidden and the person will continue to be tormented.

For years I was doing deliverance, but I didn't know how to get people free from the sexual spirits. I would get them partially, but not totally, free; some demons would remain behind. One day I had a case where I had to pray and fast in order to get someone free, and the Lord showed me that sexual spirits usually have these blocking spirits, and the blocking spirits prevent the sexual spirits from being discovered. I learned how to discover the blocking spirits, and access the sexual spirits, to get past their defense, and get the spirits out. Since then I have literally seen thousands of people freed from sexual abuse spirits and their tormenting symptoms because the Lord showed me how to do this through prayer and fasting.*

Here is the essential principle: Once the Lord handed me this "key to the kingdom," I never again needed to pray and fast to get rid of sexual spirits. Now I know how to utilize that kingdom key and unshackle people who have been abused. This is what it looks like to develop spiritual authority; this is what Jesus was teaching his disciples that day.

---

* If you are looking for deliverance, or training on how to do deliverance, I have three helpful resources. I teach through deliverance in *Soul Care* (both in my book and my video). I regularly do Soul Care Conferences where people can get free. Finally, I also have a deliverance training video that gives extremely practical help in doing deliverance in which I pass on many of the keys I have discovered through the years. The books, videos, and conference itinerary are available on my website, www.renewalinternational.org.

When we face a mountain we do not know how to move, if we are willing to pray and fast, seek God's face, and wait on Him for wisdom, He will often give us what we need to overcome. The prayer, fasting, and listening to God's voice lead us into deeper intimacy with God, often releasing the revelatory wisdom and faith we need for victory. Persistence is necessary. Developing authority is not easy. Sadly, too often I have trained people in deliverance, they run into a difficult demonic entity, and they simply give up. I've even seen people blame the person who is being attacked by demons, saying, "You don't want to get free" or "You just keep letting them back in." In reality, the problem was the leader simply didn't have the right key in their key ring to unlock this particular situation. If, instead, they persisted, praying, fasting, and waiting on God until He gave them what they needed for the breakthrough, they could have helped the person get completely free. Jesus gave us authority over all demons so we could set the captives free.

> We can only develop authority on the front lines of battle. No one becomes a warrior in training only; one can only become a warrior on the battlefield.

We can only develop authority on the front lines of battle. No one becomes a warrior in training only; one can only become a warrior on the battlefield. The training is essential to the making of the warrior, but the development cannot be completed without active engagement on the battlefield and without some battle scars.

In my book *Soul Care* I tell the story of a man named Anson. When I met Anson in a classroom, he had been through deliverance five times before, but the demons kept coming back. The first time I sat down to do his deliverance, I knew something was wrong; I just didn't know what it was. I asked him, "Have you been through deliverance before?" He told me he had been through deliverance sessions five times, and he told me who did them; they were people with a good reputation. I said, "Something is wrong. I'm not sure what it is. But I'll do what I know how to do and, if it doesn't work, then I'll figure out what to do. But with the help of Jesus, we will get you free." I did what I knew to do, but the demons came back again. I realized I was missing something; there was a key I did not have that I needed to discover if we were going to get this man free. I prayed and fasted, and we entered another round of deliverance. We ran into the exact same demon I had confronted the first time, and I couldn't figure out why the demon came back—it didn't have any ground. ("Ground" is a legal right for the demon to remain within a person.)

I was baffled, but then the Lord gave me a word of knowledge. I heard the word "godfather." I asked Anson about his godfather and he told the story of having been born on a Chinese holiday known as the Gates of Hell. His parents, wanting to protect him from the gates of hell, took him to the temple and had the godfather dedicate him to the ancestor spirits so he would be protected. But a dedication done in any name other than Jesus is not a blessing, it is a curse—no matter the intent of the people doing the dedication. Demons never bless, they only curse. That dedication forced open the gates of hell so that every time the demons were cast out, they returned. Once we broke the curse of the dedication ceremony, and commanded the demons to leave, they never returned. Anson was free, and I had picked up a new key in my key ring. I realized that you need to break curses or demons can return.

That key led me to change my deliverance methodology to include breaking curses, and as a result I have seen many more people get free and stay free.

When we pray and fast, we discover new truths about God, His ways and doings, His kingdom, and the way the spiritual realm works. These new revelatory discoveries increase our authority. But no one is simply handed the keys to the kingdom without wrestling in battle for them. You have to be on the front lines of the battlefield; God gives keys to those who are in need of them. He doesn't give revelation so we can impress people with our knowledge. God gives keys to those who are fighting to set the captives free and willing to take risks to do so. Anson's deliverance took me multiple sessions and many hours to complete. But since discovering those keys I have been able to use them to set many other people free with similar life situations, I haven't needed to pray and fast for insight about curses again, and it didn't take me many sessions and many hours. That's the power of prayer and fasting; that's the power of developing authority. This is what Jesus meant. He didn't mean some kinds of demons only come out by prayer and fasting; he meant prayer and fasting is utterly essential to developing spiritual authority so you can get people free.

When you spend years on the battlefield seeking to advance the kingdom of God against the gates of hell, you have to pray and fast for victories. This is how you keep adding keys to your key ring, and it's also how you keep developing spiritual authority. My friend Martin Sanders teaches with me at times at the Soul Care Conferences. When I teach about deliverance and model it for people, Martin often remarks, "He makes this look easier than it is. It isn't this easy."

While that's true, it wasn't "this easy" for me in the beginning either. I wasn't born with a developed spiritual authority and a big set of kingdom keys just handed to me. I wasn't handed the level of discernment I have now; that too was developed over time. I developed authority on the front lines; I developed authority in battles where I was over my head and had no idea what to do; I developed authority through prayer and fasting for wisdom and breakthroughs.

I had to develop authority like Moses, like the disciples, and like you.

Developing Authority

So how do we develop authority? I go back to the key phrase we need to explore: *Spiritual authority is rooted in identity, expanded in intimacy, and activated by faith.* We can see this statement lived out by the disciples. We already know that Jesus gave them authority to drive out demons and heal the sick. Then he sent them out to the front lines of battle because you can't develop authority by reading a book or sitting in a classroom or watching someone else do the works of the kingdom. You have to get into the cosmic battle against the kingdom of darkness.

In Luke 10, after the seventy-two followers come back from a successful mission, they report to Jesus with joy, "Even the demons submit to us in your name." Jesus responds, "I saw Satan fall like lightning from heaven. I have given you authority to trample on snakes and scorpions and to overcome all the power of the enemy; nothing will harm you. However, do not rejoice that the spirits submit to you, but *rejoice that your names are written in heaven*" (Luke 10:17-20). The disciples are rejoicing in success, they are rejoicing in the fruit, they are rejoicing in their newly given authority to overcome dark spirits. But Jesus redirects them to rejoice in the fact that they belong to the Father; their names are written in Heaven and they are children of God. He calls them to focus on their identity, not their activity. Why? Because when we focus on our activity, on our fruit-bearing, we can easily make it too much about us. We make it about our abilities, our competencies, our

> It is about authority, not ability. It is about relationship, not results. It's about the Master, not the ministry. Spiritual authority is rooted in identity. Jesus was calling them to grow deep roots.

fruit, our success. This isn't about us. It is about Christ in us, and us in Christ. It isn't about our results, it is about His kingdom. Authority comes from relationship. It is about authority, not ability. It is about relationship, not results. It's about the Master, not the ministry. Spiritual authority is rooted in identity. Jesus was calling them to grow deep roots.

Kingdom exploits are always done in Jesus' name, as Jesus' ambassadors, as sons and daughters of the King. Authority is the right to use someone else's power. The classic illustration is a police officer. When you see a police officer standing in the road with her hand up, you stop. It isn't that she has more power than you as you drive along in your SUV. You have far more power; she is standing there unprotected. But she has authority. That officer has a relationship with the government; she carries the badge, and her name and the name of the government have been united. That officer acts and speaks on behalf of the government, so when she holds up her hand, you stop. That's authority.

If we are going to develop our authority, we must be rooted in our identity in Christ. We must sink deep roots in Christ. It isn't enough just to know about our identity in Christ or to quote it or declare it. We must get to the place where we believe we are Christ's representatives on earth, we are His body, His family, His sons and daughters. We speak and act on His behalf. We have been sent out to do His bidding in His name for His glory. We are going to carefully examine our identity in Christ as it relates to authority, and we are going to talk about how to strengthen our identity so we can expand our authority.

Spiritual authority is rooted in identity and *expanded in intimacy*. Thus, when the disciples cannot cast out the demon, Jesus tells them that they need to pray and fast. Mark 9:29: "This kind can only come out by prayer" (some translations: "and fasting"). When you hit the wall of your limited knowledge and bump up against the limits of your level of authority, then you will have to pray and fast to expand your intimacy. In the expansion of your intimacy, you will come into a new level of authority.

This is something Moses discovered as well. When he was wrestling with the question "Who am I?" the Lord told him, "I will be with you." He discovered that the one irrepressible need of his life to accomplish the impossible assignment God gave him was the presence of God. When it comes to authority it is far more important that you understand who God is, and who you are to God, than it is that you understand your abilities or competencies. If you understand your gifting, but have an assignment that goes beyond your ability, you will feel like Moses: "Who am I?" If you are trying to accomplish a

God-sized assignment, it is far more about spiritual authority than it is about human ability. It is more about His presence and less about your prowess. Moses realized that he had to pursue the face of God and draw near to God if he was going to do the impossible assignment God had given him. Only God can do the impossible. We need His presence. When you understand who you are in Christ and the access you have to the throne room, and you understand who God is and that He welcomes you to act on His behalf for His kingdom and His glory, you expand your authority and increase kingdom activity. Hell is dismantled.

The disciples, too, had to learn to draw near. They had to learn to pursue intimacy. Jesus told them that if they would abide, they would bear much fruit, but that apart from Him they could do nothing (John 15). When they ran into the boy whose deliverance they could not bring about, Jesus told them they needed to pray and fast. They had to expand their intimacy. It wasn't enough just to know their identity; they had to go deeper, they had to draw nearer. Abiding, drawing near, and remaining closely connected to Jesus were vital to seeing the demonstrations of kingdom power that Jesus expected the disciples to move in. They couldn't do it because they were gifted, talented, or capable people. Demonstrations of supernatural power flow through intimacy, not ability.

The closer we draw to God, the more of His presence we carry, the more we know the mind of Christ and pray it into being with confidence. A bit later, we will do a deeper dive into intimacy with God and how it relates to our expanding authority. But know this for now: we will have to pay the price for intimacy, just as Moses and the disciples had to, if we want to expand our authority.

Spiritual authority is rooted in identity, expanded in intimacy, and *activated by faith*. Mark emphasized prayer and fasting, but Matthew highlights the need to activate authority through faith. When the disciples couldn't drive out the demon, Jesus said, "Truly I tell you, if you have faith as small as a mustard seed, you can say to this mountain, 'Move from here to there,' and it will move. Nothing will be impossible for you" (Matthew 17:20).

Jesus uses a formulaic expression with his disciples: "truly I tell you." Literally, this is "truly, truly." This is an expression that Jesus only uses when He is about to release a revelation on a group of people He knows will dismiss it out of hand because it seems so incredible. He drops a "double truly" on them. It's as if Jesus is saying to them, and us, "Listen, I know that you are going to want to dismiss what I am about to say because it seems too good to be true, but I am telling you that this is doubly true. Truly, truly. You can take this one to God's eternal bank. If you would only believe, you would live to see it."

When Jesus drops a "double truly," He is trying to overcome our natural resistance to His supernatural truth. This double truly promise states that if we believe we can move mountains, nothing will be impossible for us. But this mountain-moving faith is connected to authority because it is by authority that Jesus told them they could drive out demons. And if we are going to act in mountain-moving authority, we must activate our faith. Authority without faith is like a car without an engine—it doesn't go. Faith that moves mountains cannot be passive faith, it cannot be underdeveloped faith; it must be an active, mature faith in the barrier-breaking, earth-moving power of God. Faith, too, like understanding our identity and growing in intimacy and maturity and authority, is developmental.

We are going to look at how to develop authority that can move the mountains in our life. But before we do, we need to take a deeper look at Jesus, His message, and His ministry because Jesus, too, operated from authority.

He led the way. Let's learn from Him in the next chapter.

Three:
Jesus' Message
and Ministry

Jesus is our model for life and ministry. If you want to know what God is like, look to Jesus. If you want to know how to connect deeply with the Father, look to Jesus. If you want to know how to live a life pleasing to God, look to Jesus. If you want to know how to do ministry, look to Jesus.

My philosophy of ministry has always been very simple: We should do the things Jesus did. Jesus cast out demons, healed the sick, saved the lost, and set the captives free. So that's the stuff we ought to do. That is kingdom normal, but it isn't always "church normal." When the church isn't operating in kingdom normal, that's because the church is *abnormal*. Jesus hasn't changed, and neither has His mission.

Sometimes we say we believe the things the Bible says like, "Jesus Christ is the same yesterday and today and forever" (Hebrews 13:8). But then we don't live that out. And yet we see no disconnect between what we say we believe and the way we live. It has always bothered me when I read things in the Bible that aren't being lived out in my life and in the church; I always feel compelled to close the gap.

The Gospel of the Kingdom

If we are going to look to Jesus as a model for ministry, we need to start by looking at Jesus' message, because His ministry was directly connected to His message. Jesus' central message was about the kingdom of God. It was the first thing Jesus talked about! "Repent, for the kingdom of heaven has come near" (Matthew 4:17). It was the last thing Jesus talked to His disciples about: "He appeared to them over a period of forty days and spoke about the kingdom of God" (Acts 1:3). And in between these times, Jesus' teaching was constantly focused on the kingdom. So many of Jesus' parables are about the kingdom and start with phrases like, "The kingdom of God is like . . . " (Take a look at these verses: Mark 4:26; Matthew 13:24, 31, 45, 47; Matthew 22:2; Luke 13:18).

Everywhere Jesus went He proclaimed the "good news of the kingdom." When we talk about preaching the gospel, we do not usually associate it with the *gospel of the kingdom*. All too often we have reduced the gospel message to this: "We are sinners separated from God, Jesus came and lived a sinless life, died on the cross for the forgiveness of our sins and rose again, and if we put our faith in Christ we are forgiven, made right with God, and have eternal life." And all that is absolutely true. But that is not the full message of the good news of the kingdom that Jesus preached. It is only part of the message. Since the gospel of the kingdom is clearly the central message of Jesus, we ought to be able to quickly and clearly articulate what the kingdom is.

Notice these summary statements in the Matthew's gospel. Matthew 4:23, 24: "Jesus went throughout Galilee, teaching in their synagogues, proclaiming the good news of the kingdom, and healing every disease and sickness among the people. News about him spread all over Syria, and people brought to him all who were ill with various diseases, those suffering severe pain, the demon-possessed, those having seizures, and the paralyzed; and he healed them."

Matthew 9:35-38: "Jesus went through all the towns and villages, teaching in their synagogues, proclaiming the good news of the kingdom and healing every disease and sickness. When he saw crowds, he had compassion on them, because they were harassed and helpless, like sheep without a shepherd. Then he said to his disciples, 'The harvest is plentiful, but the workers are few. Ask the Lord of the harvest, therefore, to send out workers into his harvest field.'" And in the very next scene, Jesus sends out the Twelve and gives them authority to drive out demons and heal the sick as they proclaim the good news of the kingdom (Matthew 10:1-8). Matthew 10:1, 7: "Jesus called his twelve disciples to him and gave them authority to drive out impure spirits and to heal every disease and sickness . . . 'As you go, proclaim this message: "The kingdom of heaven has come near." Heal the sick, raise the dead, cleanse those who have leprosy, drive out demons. Freely you have received; freely give.'"

These summary statements indicate that everywhere Jesus went He preached the gospel of the kingdom, cast out demons, and healed the sick. Then He told the disciples to proclaim

> Everywhere Jesus went He preached the gospel of the kingdom, cast out demons, and healed the sick.

the same message and do the same things. *There is no proc-lamation of the gospel of the kingdom in the New Testament without a demonstration of power.* When the kingdom comes, the manifestations of the kingdom are visible. It is an invisible kingdom with visible results. How can we convincingly proclaim a King who has heavenly power without a demonstration of that power to undo the works of hell?

So, what is the gospel of the kingdom, clearly and concisely stated? *The kingdom of God is the reversal of everything that went wrong with the world when sin entered the world. It is the restoration of the way things were supposed to be.* The kingdom deals with sin and its impact on our planet. The apostle John wrote, "The reason the Son of God appeared was to destroy the devil's work" (1 John 3:8). Sin, and all its evil manifestations, is the work of the devil; Jesus came to reverse that, to restore the way of Heaven on earth. That's the kingdom. It is an invasion of Heaven's ways on hell's turf. The deaf hear, the mute talk, the lame walk, the demonized are delivered, the brokenhearted are mended, broken relationships are restored, justice is served, and the spiritually lost are found. There is no proper proclamation of the kingdom without a demonstration of heavenly power that destroys the devil's works and overturns evil. When Jesus came preaching that the kingdom of God was at hand, He demonstrated the reality of the message by healing the sick and casting out demons. Sickness and demonization were marks of Satan's kingdom that Jesus came to destroy.

If we are going to understand the kingdom, we need to understand the larger picture. When God created Adam and Eve, He handed them a kingdom. He gave them dominion, or rulership. God is sovereign, so human beings, created in the image of God, are created with a degree of sovereignty. This means at least two things: first, we were created for rulership under God's rulership. We were designed to rule in submission to God, to advance His kingdom here on earth as it is in Heaven. Second, since a sovereign being has choice, we have choice. God has ultimate choice; we have limited choice. God wants us to bring our choices under His sovereign rule so we can co-rule with Him as sons and daughters and ambassadors in His kingdom. As we bring our choices in alignment with God's choices, we can rule under God's reign. Our submission to the King gives us a right to use the King's power to advance the kingdom as we operate in His authority. But we can only operate in authority to the degree that we are in submission to the King.

> We are spiritual beings in a spiritual world; we are always giving away spiritual access. The only question is: to whom are we giving access?

When Satan tempted Adam and Eve and they sinned, they forfeited the keys to the kingdom. They had rebelled against the King and stepped out of alignment with God. They forfeited their authority as they stepped out of submission to God. Scripture says that, as a result, Satan is "ruler of the kingdom of the air" (Ephesians 2:2). He is called the "god of this age" (2 Corinthians 4:4). Jesus called him the "prince of this world" (John 14:30). Satan is now seeking to extend his tyrannical rule of evil on the planet. He is king of the kingdom of darkness, and he extends the kingdom of darkness through the deeds of darkness: sin, evil, sickness, demonization, and death are just some of the visible manifestations of his kingdom. Satan brings pain, terror, torment, and bondage. Jesus brings healing, love, fullness, and freedom.

We are spiritual beings in a spiritual world; we are always giving away spiritual access. The only question is: to whom are we giving access? Satan tempts us to pick up the tools of the kingdom of darkness rather than submitting ourselves to God's rule and picking up the tools of the kingdom of light. When we use the tools of the kingdom of darkness, we are giving access to the enemy of our souls. We cannot use the tools of darkness to gain freedom in the kingdom of light. Rebellion, for example, is a tool of darkness. Jesus submitted Himself to God because, as servant of all, He perfectly obeyed the Father's will. But Adam and Eve picked up the tools of darkness when they rebelled against God's word and ate the fruit, giving access to the enemy. His dark kingdom began to pervade their lives: sickness, demonization, division, injustice, and death entered the world. The world fell under the dominion of darkness, and its evil impact is felt all around us still.

Every time we pick up the tool of rebellion, we are picking up a tool of darkness, and it can only lead to bondage, never freedom. For example, if someone sins against us and hurts us, Jesus tells us to forgive them, to bless those who curse us (Luke 6:27, 28). If we forgive, we pick up the tool of the kingdom of God, we give access to God. If we hold on to bitterness, we are picking up the tool of the kingdom of Satan and we are giving access to Satan. Paul says that the devil gets a foothold (Eph 4:27f), ground—he gets access. Humanity is locked in Satan's dark kingdom and its effects because we have all sinned and given Satan access. So our lives are saturated with the fruits of darkness: pain, suffering, sorrow, injustice, sickness, demonization, bondage, addiction, poverty, and the like.

These things were not part of God's design in the beginning, and they will not be found in Heaven.

After the fall, we were all under the reign of Satan and the kingdom of darkness, but then Jesus came. He submitted himself perfectly to the Father's will. He was the "last Adam," a life-giving Spirit; he was the "second man," the man from Heaven (1 Corinthians 15:45-48). He took back the keys to the kingdom that were rightfully given to image-bearing humanity but had been usurped by Satan. Jesus gave those keys of the kingdom to the church, to the redeemed people of God; He restored the kingdom back to its rightful recipients. "I confer on you a kingdom, just as my Father conferred one on me" (Luke 22:29).

In Matthew 16:18, 19, Jesus said, "And I tell you that you are Peter, and on this rock I will build my church, and the gates of Hades will not overcome it. I will give you the keys of the kingdom of heaven; whatever you bind on earth will be bound in heaven, and whatever you loose on earth will be loosed in heaven." The keys to the kingdom and the mission of the kingdom were entrusted to God's redeemed people so they could extend the manifestations of the kingdom throughout the earth and take back the territory of the kingdom of Satan, overthrow his dark reign, and undo his evil works. They could extend the works of Jesus as His hands and feet, His body, and continue to destroy the works of the devil in Jesus' name.

The kingdom of God is not merely manifest in sinners being saved, but also in the works of the devil being destroyed and as the invasion of Heaven on our sin-stained and evil-tainted planet. Healing, deliverance, justice, reconciliation, liberty to the captives, freedom, and fullness are all parts of the salvation Jesus came to offer. The kingdom of God is the reversal of everything that went wrong when sin entered the world; it is the restoration of the way God intended things to be. It is the overthrow of the kingdom of hell and establishment of God's ways and doings on our planet. And the kingdom was *conferred on people like us.* But we cannot advance this glorious kingdom with human ability alone; we must utilize the authority that is ours in Christ so we can demonstrate the King's power in the cosmic battle against evil. It is a spiritual kingdom that is released and revealed through spiritual authority.

The kingdom of Heaven is a superior realm to the kingdom of hell. Light always dispels darkness; you cannot turn up the darkness to snuff out light. Of course, Heaven's King is the superior king; Jesus is the King of kings and Lord of lords. He is the Creator who spoke everything into existence; all other things are inferior created beings and ultimately subject to His final judgment. He has no competition for His throne room. Therefore, when we proclaim the King and His kingdom, it should come with a demonstration of Heaven's power to invade and overthrow hell. It should clearly and visibly demonstrate Heaven's superiority over hell's current reign on earth.

The Works of Jesus

I grew up going to church. For most of my life I heard preachers say that Jesus did His miracles because He was God. In other words, He did His miracles out of His divinity. I do not believe this is true. I believe Jesus did His miracles out of His Spirit-anointed humanity, and these works were signs that pointed to His Sonship. He did His miracles in spiritual authority, showing us the way to demonstrate the kingdom and validate the message of the kingdom.

In Philippians 2:5-8, Paul wrote, "In your relationships with one another, have the same attitude of mind as Christ

Jesus had: Who, being in very nature God, did not consider equality with God something to be used to his own advantage; rather, he made himself nothing by taking the very nature of a servant, being made in human likeness. And being found in appearance as a human being, he humbled himself by becoming obedient to death—even death on a cross!" The phrase here translated "used to his own advantage" literally means "grasped"; it is the act of seizing something. Jesus did not cling to His right to use His divine attributes; rather, He "made himself nothing." Literally: "He emptied himself." He never ceased to be divine; He did not empty Himself of His divinity. He emptied Himself of His right to use His divine attributes. When Jesus was on the planet, for example, He didn't access His omnipresence; He limited himself to one place at one time. He was still divine, but He chose not to use His divine right to be everywhere at once. When Jesus was on the planet, He chose not to use His omniscience. He asked the disciples questions. When He knew things supernaturally, He knew those things through the Spirit; He was dependent on the Father for that revelation of supernatural knowledge. He was operating in spiritual gifts like prophecy (hearing God's voice), gaining supernatural insight from God in the same manner that we do.

While He was on the planet, He ministered as a human who was filled with the Spirit. He served in complete obedience to the Father. As the last Adam, He did what the first Adam was supposed to do. Jesus did not do miracles because He was choosing to use His divine power; Jesus did miracles because He was obedient to His Father and did His Father's bidding with the Spirit's empowerment. He did the acts of the kingdom by the authority the Father gave Him. He was enacting the Father's rule, just as Adam was supposed to, by bringing His life in alignment with the Father and doing the Father's bidding.

The Gospel of John makes an overwhelming case that Jesus didn't use His divine nature to do miracles, but that everything He did was in dependence on the Father. Let's dive down and take a closer look.

In John 4 Jesus told His disciples, "I have food to eat that you know nothing about. . . . My food is to do the will of him who sent me and to finish his work" (John 4:32-34). This was the key to Jesus' ministry—every day, every moment, every encounter, Jesus sought to do the will of His Father. The key question for Jesus was, "What is the Father doing?" Then in every situation, He simply joined the Father in what He was doing. Fulfilling the Father's desire was food to Jesus' soul. It gave Him pleasure and replenished His soul. When we try to generate spiritual activity out of our ability without the empowerment of the Spirit, it drains us quickly. The acts of the kingdom must come through the presence of God. Moses discovered this; he had to seek God's face, enter God's glory, and access spiritual authority to accomplish his assignment. The disciples discovered this; they had to abide and use the authority Jesus had given them. Jesus was the One who showed us the way. He came to do the Father's will and work, and He did it through His union with the Father.

> When we try to generate spiritual activity out of our ability without the empowerment of the Spirit, it drains us quickly. The acts of the kingdom must come through the presence of God.

Beginning in John 5:19, Jesus said, "Very truly I tell you, the Son can do nothing by himself; he can do only what he sees his Father doing, because whatever the Father does the Son also does. For the Father loves the Son and shows him all he does." In John 5:30, Jesus said, "By myself I can do nothing; I judge only as I hear, and my judgment is just, for I seek not to please myself but him who sent me." Twice in these verses Jesus says He can do nothing by Himself; He is in complete submission to His Father. If He were acting in His divinity, He would have the power to do divine acts. But Jesus, fulfilling His role as the last Adam, emptied Himself of His right to use His divine attributes on His own. So that, apart from the Father, Jesus could do nothing. He couldn't do the miracles on His own because He chose to identify with us so thoroughly; He laid aside the right to use His divine attributes. He attuned himself to the Father's activity, then joined the Father and accomplished the works of the kingdom by the power of the Spirit. The Father showed Jesus what He was doing, and Jesus joined in bringing about the kingdom.

Jesus not only said He could do nothing on his own, He also taught that He could *say nothing* without the Father. John 7:16: "My teaching is not my own. It comes from the one who sent me." John 8:28: "When you have lifted up the Son of Man, then you will know that I am he and that I do nothing on my own but speak just what the Father has taught me." John 12:49, 50: "For I did not speak on my own, but the Father who sent me commanded me to say all that I have spoken. I know that his command leads to eternal life. So whatever I say is just what the Father has told me to say." John 14:10: "The words I say to you I do not speak on my own authority. Rather, it is the Father, living in me, who is doing his work." John 14:24: "These words you hear are not my own; they belong to the

Father who sent me." Jesus spoke with such weighty words because His words came from the Father. They were words of revelation that came from Heaven, and everyone whose heart was soft and listened could feel the eternal, ancient weightiness of His words. These words emerged from His union with the Father. He spoke with authority, unlike the rest of the teachers of His day, because His words came not from human wisdom but from Heaven's revelation.

Jesus lived in complete submission to the Father. He only did what the Father told Him to do. He only judged as the Father told Him to judge. He only said what the Father told Him to say. He only went where the Father told Him to go. Jesus didn't cleverly invent His teachings; He didn't know all of these great spiritual insights as a baby. (Though, even then, He was fully God and fully human.) He had to walk in alignment with, and in submission to, His Father. As He did, insights came and His authority expanded. He did it all perfectly, so no one has ever lived or will ever live with His level of authority.

When Jesus chose to leave Heaven and become a man, He laid aside His right to access these divine attributes. When the enemy tempted Jesus, part of that temptation was that Jesus use His divine attributes for His own benefit (Matthew 4). But Jesus wouldn't; He would not use His divine power to turn stones to bread even though He was extremely hungry. He wouldn't get out of sync with His Father's desires for His life. Jesus responded that man does not live by bread alone but by every word that proceeds from the mouth of the Father (Matthew 4:4).

The Father is the source of eternal life. The Father is the source of Heaven's power to overcome hell's tyranny. Hearing and obeying the Father releases the life of the Father to those in alignment with Him. The first Adam was duped by Satan and rebelled against the Father, but the second Adam lived only on the Father's will. He only gave access to the Father, and in doing so He gained access to the resources of Heaven. When we give access to God, we gain access to the things of God. The kingdom of Heaven invaded everywhere Jesus went as a result of this access to Heaven.

Jesus was dependent on the Father for power, wisdom, insight, and revelation. The Father and He were one. The Father lived in Jesus and Jesus lived in the Father, and their divine union was the key to His kingdom fruit-bearing. Jesus was modeling for us how to live a kingdom life in authority. He didn't live a kingdom life in His divinity. That would be unattainable to us. But He showed us the way of authority, through abiding, through access, through submission and obedience, and then He deposited His Spirit in us so we could follow His example.

Partnering with Jesus

We are to carry on the ministry of Jesus. We are to proclaim the message of Jesus, the gospel of the kingdom. We need to follow His footsteps. We have the Spirit of Jesus living in us, and we can operate in authority, like Jesus did, in dependence on the Father, and demonstrate the gospel of the kingdom that we proclaim, just like Jesus. This is Jesus' plan. This is why Jesus chastised

This is Jesus' plan. This is why Jesus chastised the disciples for their puny faith and called them to mountain-moving, authority-exercising faith that could demonstrate the kingdom.

the disciples for their puny faith and called them to mountain-moving, authority-exercising faith that could demonstrate the kingdom.

All of this isn't my idea; Jesus taught it. In John 14:12-14, Jesus said, "Very truly I tell you, all who have faith in me will do the works I have been doing, and they will do even greater things than these, because I am going to the Father. And I will do whatever you ask in my name, so that the Father may be glorified in the Son. You may ask me for anything in my name, and I will do it." Jesus employs that double truly again—"truly, truly"—because He is about to drop a revelation bomb in the room that people are going to start to pull away from and explain away because it seems too ridiculous to be true. "All"— that is the scope of the promise. "Who have faith in me"—that is the condition of the promise. "Will do the works I have been doing"—that is the promise. We will do the things Jesus did. The word "works" is John's technical term for the works of the kingdom. We will proclaim the message Jesus proclaimed and demonstrate the works Jesus demonstrated, but we have to do it the way Jesus did: in total dependence on the Father, in intimacy with the Father, and with spiritual authority granted by the Father.

The one thing God most wants is access. We are spiritual beings in a spiritual world, so we are always giving away spiritual access. God simply wants us to trust Him and give access to Him—and when we do, we gain access to the resources of Heaven. Then we can appropriate Heaven's victories and make the kingdom manifest; we appropriate Heaven's victories by utilizing the tools of the kingdom. For example, when I am hurt, God wants me to forgive those who sin against me, bless those who curse me, and love my enemies. The enemy wants me to rehearse the offense, nurse a grudge, and hold on to bitterness. I don't get to choose *if* I give away access; I only get to choose to whom I will give access. If I pick up the tools of the kingdom of light and bless those who curse me and forgive those who sin against me, I give access to God. Then I gain access to the victory of Jesus. If you obey God and do what He tells you to do, God will do what you cannot do: change your heart. He will give you access to the victories over bitterness in the heavenly realms (there is no bitterness in Heaven) and your heart will begin to move toward loving your enemy in a supernatural move of the Spirit.

1 John 1:5, 6 says, "God is light; in him there is no darkness at all. If we claim to have fellowship with him and yet walk in the darkness, we lie and do not live out the truth." God never shines light into the suitcase of our souls to make us feel bad; he does so to get us free. For example, He shines light into our souls to show us we are struggling with envy. But if we deny that truth, if we explain it away, we are not giving God access to our souls. We are denying the light God offers and we are giving the enemy access by continuing to deny our envious ways. We are picking up a tool of the kingdom of darkness, hiding, and reaping the results of that darkness in our lives. John says that by denying the truth that God shows us, we lie and do not live out the truth. God doesn't want us to only believe the truth; He wants us to live out the truth. This is integration. We cannot live out the truth while we are picking up the tools of the kingdom of darkness. We have to integrate truth into our lives by giving God access and picking up the tools of the kingdom of light and living them out.

We need to access the victories of Jesus to live the kingdom life. Not only did Jesus teach that apart from the Father He could do nothing, He taught that apart from Him we could do nothing. He lived it, and He called us into it. He gave access and gained access to the Father's power for kingdom demonstration. In John 15:5 Jesus said, "I am the vine; you are the branches. If you remain in me and I in you, you will bear much fruit; apart from me you can do nothing." Here is the key to demonstrating the kingdom: we must abide. Authority flows from relationship. In John 10:30, Jesus said, "I and the Father are one." It was His divine union with the Father that gave Him the right to act for the Father. It was His total submission and intimacy that gave Him authority to cast out demons, heal the sick, and set captives free. As we abide in Christ, He can bear the fruit in us that the Father bore in Him through their intimate connection.

In Mark 1:22 Jesus goes into a synagogue and begins to teach. Note how Mark describes this scene: "The people were amazed at his teaching, because he taught them as one who had authority, not as the teachers of the law." Jesus' words were marked with the Father's presence, thus bringing a weightiness to them; they demonstrated His authority. Everybody could feel the weightiness of His revelatory words. He wasn't a man of mere human wisdom or insight; He was a man of authority.

But if you are going to proclaim the gospel of the kingdom—that Heaven is invading earth and hell is being dismantled—you must demonstrate it. You can't just have weighty words about Heaven's invasion without hell's disruption. You must show the reality of the message you proclaim with a demonstration of Heaven's power. Heaven must show up. "Just then a man in their synagogue who was possessed by an evil spirit cried out, 'What do you want with us, Jesus of Nazareth? Have you come to destroy us? I know who you are—the Holy One of God!' 'Be quiet!' said Jesus sternly. 'Come out of him!' The evil spirit shook the man violently and came out of him with a shriek. The people were all so amazed that they asked each other, 'What is this? A new teaching—and with authority! He even gives orders to evil spirits and they obey him'" (Mark 1:23-27).

Jesus proclaimed the gospel of the kingdom with weighty words that came from revelation through abiding. And He demonstrated the gospel of the kingdom with supernatural power that set captives free.

Identity, Intimacy, and Faith in Jesus

I stated that spiritual authority is rooted in identity, expanded in intimacy, and activated by faith. Let's look at this a bit more in the life of Jesus. At Jesus' baptism, before He had done any public ministry, there is an incredible scene that unfolds. Beginning in 3:16, Matthew writes, "As soon as Jesus was baptized, he went up out of the water. At that moment heaven was opened, and he saw the Spirit of God descending like a dove and alighting on him. And a voice from heaven said, 'This is my Son, whom I love; with him I am well pleased.'"

> Jesus holds on to the revelation of the Father; He doesn't waver. He is being rooted in His identity. To be rooted in our identity it is necessary for our identity to be tested.

Jesus is about to launch into His public ministry, and the first thing He hears from the Father concerns His identity. Twice that we know of, Jesus hears the audible voice of His Father (here at His baptism and at His transfiguration) and both times the Father speaks to Him about His identity.

Immediately, Jesus is led by the Spirit into the wilderness, and there He is tempted by the enemy. The enemy begins his temptation by attacking Jesus' identity: "If you are the Son of God . . . " (Matthew 4:3). Jesus holds on to the revelation of the Father; He doesn't waver. He is being rooted in His identity. To be rooted in our identity it is necessary for our identity to be tested. In the first temptation in this scene, Satan says, "If you are the Son of God, tell these stones to become bread." Jesus was on a long fast and the temptation was to use His divine attributes without the Father's prompting for His own gain. Jesus quickly responds: "It is written: 'People do not live on bread alone, but on every word that comes from the mouth of God'" (Matthew 4:4). Jesus claims the Word to solidify and deepen the word He has just heard from the Father. He holds on to the revelation. Spiritual authority is rooted in identity. Identity can't be rooted without revelation, nor without testing.

Jesus is in the wilderness fasting for forty days. He had been led there by the Spirit (Matthew 4:1). It is in this time of fasting that He is tested and tempted. Prayer, fasting, testing, and temptation are essential for deepening intimacy, and expanding intimacy is necessary for developing authority. Luke says that Jesus, who had just experienced the dove descend on Him at His baptism, went into the wilderness filled with the Spirit. "Jesus, full of the Holy Spirit, left the Jordan and was led by the Spirit into the wilderness" (Luke 4:1). But Luke goes on to tell us that after this time of prayer and fasting, tempting and testing, Jesus returned in the power of the Spirit (Luke 4:14). Again: *spiritual authority is rooted in identity and expanded in intimacy.* This is where the power of God starts to mark Jesus' life. He is operating in authority.

We know from our study in John that Jesus only does what the Father tells Him to do. His total submission to the Father demonstrates His utter trust; whatever the Father tells Him to do, He simply obeys. (Remember: spiritual authority is rooted in identity, expanded in intimacy, and activated by faith.) Jesus only does what the Father tells Him to do; He only goes where the Father tells Him to go; He only says what the Father tells Him to say. He is completely at rest in doing the Father's will because of His deep faith. Doing the Father's will was food for His soul. James tells us that faith without deeds is dead, but Jesus has an active faith; His faith always leads to faithfulness. His faith always leads to obedience. Biblically speaking, the opposite of faith is not doubt; the opposite of faith is *disobedience*. Jesus demonstrates faith that leads to deeds; He did whatever the Father asked of Him. And the results were astounding.

His faith always leads to obedience. Biblically speaking, the opposite of faith is not doubt; the opposite of faith is disobedience.

Seeing Hell Break Apart

Jesus calls us to follow in His footsteps: to abide in Him and act with spiritual authority. Gary Thomas, in his book *Seeking the Face of God*, wrote, "Jesus chased out ignorance, defeated the demonic, and released the ill and oppressed. In other words, as Jesus walked, hell broke apart at His feet. Jesus and hell could not occupy the same spot, so wherever Jesus went, hell was dismantled. Together, his life and teaching provide a clear goal—seeing hell break apart at our feet and the coming forth of the kingdom of God."[4]

I love that. Hell broke apart at Jesus' feet. This is the gospel of the kingdom and this is the goal of our life in Christ. The message of salvation is so much more than being forgiven. It includes that wonderful truth, but it includes much more. It unravels evil's thread of dark influence on our planet. It unshackles the chains of bondage that enslave humanity. It unhinges the gates of hell and sets prisoners free. It releases supernatural power for healing, freedom, deliverance, justice, reconciliation, and wholeness.

> He is a God who can help! The kingdom is the invasive and pervasive spread of God's victories to people defeated by evil.

The kingdom is not about going to church on Sunday and singing a few songs, praying together, collecting an offering, and listening to a sermon. The kingdom is the destruction of the devil's kingdom and the establishment of God's rule and reign here and now. It is a demonstration that the King is alive, that His power is a real, current, active, breakthrough power. He is a God who can help! The kingdom is the invasive and pervasive spread of God's victories to people defeated by evil. This is why Jesus told us to pray that His kingdom would come on earth as it is in Heaven. In Heaven there is not going to be any sickness. In Heaven there will not be demonized people. There will not be injustice. There will not be prejudice or racism or sexism. There will not be abuse or broken hearts. In Heaven everything that God intended for us will be fulfilled, and evil and all its effects will be done away with. God has established a redeemed people on earth to administer Heaven's victories in the here and now so people can catch a glimpse of Heaven in this dark world—to bring people lost in darkness to Heaven's King of light. We are to live in authority so people are attracted to Jesus and can see and feel what Heaven might be like in all its fullness. This is about authority, not ability. This is what Jesus did and this is what Jesus called the disciples to do with Him, and this is Jesus' plan for our lives too.

Wherever Jesus went He cast out demons, healed the sick, saved the lost, and set the captives free. That is *kingdom normal*. When Heaven invades earth, the works of the enemy are overturned. When the church no longer demonstrates the gospel of the kingdom, we have twisted the gospel we proclaim. We have reduced the gospel to something Jesus never meant it to be. The gospel must come with a demonstration of God's victorious might over Satan because Satan's grip on human lives is felt by all. When the church proclaims a gospel without power, it is because we are, all too often, operating out of human ability rather than spiritual authority. We need the presence of Christ to heal the sick, mend the wounded soul, release forgiveness to a sinner caught in shame, unite fractured relationships, and heal broken hearts. We need the presence of Christ to overcome injustice and cast out demons. When Jesus is present, lives are changed and hell breaks apart at our feet. We need to seek His face, just as Moses learned to do. We need to abide in Christ and Christ in us. We need to understand and act in genuine spiritual authority.

I cannot make the kingdom come, but I can be rooted in identity. I can't produce supernatural results, but I can pursue God's face. I can't manufacture healing power, but I can develop a deeper faith. I can only do my part, the part God asks me to do. God does the rest.

When the church fails to utilize her authority, people are left in bondage. Deliverance was a major part of Jesus' ministry.

One third of the miracle stories in the gospels were deliverance stories. Every summary statement about Jesus' ministry in the gospels includes that He preached the good news of the kingdom, cast out demons, and healed the sick. This is kingdom normal.

Yet the church has all but abandoned deliverance ministry. I am more and more convinced that we must restore this ministry of deliverance or we will be forever ineffective at addressing the bondage issues that prevent people from life change. I've taken more hits for doing deliverance than any other aspect of *Soul Care*. But I will gladly take hits from the ignorant to free the captives. I am grateful for the thousands of testimonies I have heard of the transforming power that deliverance ministry has had on lives. And I am grateful for the hundreds of people who have been equipped through Soul Care Conferences and have joined the ranks of those restoring this vital ministry to the church. We are taking back the ground of the enemy! We are stepping out in authority and dismantling hell. It is cosmic treason for the church to possess the keys of the kingdom and not utilize them to set captives free!

> It is cosmic treason for the church to possess the keys of the kingdom and not utilize them to set captives free!

The goal of ministry is to advance the Kingdom of God. God wants us to reverse the effects of the fall. He wants you to do the same things Jesus did. Jesus told us that the gates of hell would not prevail against us. He gave us the keys of the kingdom to unlock the shackles that hell and its minions have placed on people. We must learn how to develop authority and use the keys of the kingdom to set captives free. Let's next take a deeper look at how authority is developed.

Four:
Spiritual Authority Is
Rooted in Identity

Spiritual authority is rooted in identity,
expanded in intimacy, and activated by faith.

My kids have had lots of friends in the house over the years. Not uncommonly, while they are visiting, my kids will get something to eat, yet often their friends will be reluctant to indulge. While the friends may feel a little shy about eating the food, my kids are never hesitant to eat me out of house and home! When my kids can't find what they want to eat they voice their opinion without reluctance: "There is nothing to eat!" Of course, Jen and I can always find "something," but what they mean is they can't find what they *feel like* eating, that we are running low on some of their fundamental staples. They feel perfectly fine accessing whatever I have paid for because they are my children and that comes with certain privileges. They simply believe that what is mine is theirs. And that is true, because I love them and deeply desire to be generous to them and provide not only what they need but often what they *want* as well. But their friends are usually more reluctant because they are visitors; they don't feel they have that same privileged access.

The more we understand our identity as sons and daughters, the more we can feel free to approach God with boldness. We come to God with confidence, believing Him to be a good and generous Father who longs to give us more than simply what we need—He loves to display His goodness to us as well. The more we know who we are in Christ, the more we feel like we have a seat at the table, a voice in the room, a position of belonging. We pray with more faith when we believe we have this kind of privileged access.

> The more we know who we are in Christ, the more we feel like we have a seat at the table, a voice in the room, a position of belonging.

We cannot develop greater spiritual authority without expanded revelation of our identity in Christ. It is not enough to know who we are in Christ or to *declare* who we are in Christ; this must be made known to us through the revelation of the Holy Spirit. When the disciples cast out demons, they were thrilled and said to Jesus, "Even the demons submit to us in your name." Jesus celebrated with them, but He also said to them, "Do not rejoice that the spirits submit to you but rejoice that your names are written in heaven" (Luke 10:17-20).

Jesus wants them to rejoice in their identity, not in their ministry success. Focusing on their success has the potential of making it too much about them; the more they make it about them, the more they will only be able to do what humans can do. The more we understand that we belong to God, that we are His children, the more we will act on His behalf as family members. Children who know they are well loved act with privileged access because they belong to the family; they carry the family name.

> Children who know they are well loved act with privileged access because they belong to the family; they carry the family name.

The writer of Hebrews said, "Therefore, since we have a great high priest who has ascended into heaven, Jesus the Son of God, let us hold firmly to the faith we profess. For we do not have a high priest who is unable to empathize with our weaknesses, but we have one who has been tempted in every way, just as we are—yet he did not sin. Let us then approach God's throne of grace with confidence, so that we may receive mercy and find grace to help us in our time of need" (Hebrews 4:14-16). When we know we belong as family, we are brave to ask the Father for what we need. That's what family does. But when we still have soul issues that make us feel like outsiders, we don't approach the Father with this same confidence. Our underdeveloped sense of identity makes us feel like beggars, visitors, and guests, not children, and it erodes our faith in God's keen willingness to respond to us. It also diminishes our confidence to trust God in the dark times. When we are walking in the fresh revelation of our status as adopted children of God, we believe God can redeem the hardships of life for our good. But it is hard to trust Him in the dark when we are not in the light about who we are.

As I am completing the final edit of this book our world has been shaken by the coronavirus, COVID-19. People have been seized with fear of sickness and death. But more than that our social isolation has caused us to shut down the world economy and, here in the US, 30 million people have filed for unemployment in just six weeks. We have never seen anything like it. I am convinced that we stand at the precipice of an un-precedented kingdom opportunity. Seldom has revival come in times of comfort, ease, and prosperity. Revival has most often birthed out of pain, famine, war, and persecution. God redeems hardship in our lives personally and corporately. But He can only redeem it to the degree we trust Him and surren-der to His shaping hand. This is a time for the church to lean into God and be purified so that we can shine the bright light of the kingdom into the darkness of the hour. We must walk in the light of who we are as dearly loved children, citizens of Heaven, to capture the redemptive potential of this historic kingdom moment.

Moses' identity issues impaired his spiritual authority; his shame made him hide his face from God. As long as he felt he needed to hide from God, he could never live out the poten-tial he had as a son. As he pur-sued God's presence, his shame was healed, and his confidence to approach God boldly grew. He moved from outsider to in-sider, from orphan to son, from beggar to family member. As his identity was strengthened, his intimacy went deeper and

> The greatest gap in most of our Christian lives is between that which is known and that which has not yet been made known by the Holy Spirit through revelation.

his authority developed. It isn't enough to know that we are dearly loved children of God; that must be made known to us by the Holy Spirit. The greatest gap in most of our Christian lives is between that which is known and that which has not yet been made known by the Holy Spirit through revelation. Only when we have the Spirit's revelation that we are deeply loved children of God will we approach the throne of grace boldly like people with privileged access.

Ephesus: A Case Study in Authority

Let's take a closer look at our identity as it relates to our authority. And then let's examine how to strengthen our identity in Christ so we can develop our authority. I want to begin by using the church at Ephesus as a case study in authority.

Ephesus was a fairly sophisticated, educated place, a city quite large for its day; it was a pluralistic, syncretistic city. There were over fifty different deities worshiped in this city, and the chief deity was Dianna, also known as Artemis of the Ephesians. She was known as the Queen of Heaven. Artemis was called both lord and savior—they used the exact words for her that we use for Jesus in the Greek language. Paul came to town preaching that Jesus was Lord and Savior, and that the church had been born. That just led to a problem. People didn't go all in, exclusively, for Jesus only; they added Jesus to their plethora of deities. They were syncretistic: they were used to worshiping many deities, so they simply added Jesus to the mix. Artemis was their real "lord and savior." So, in their minds, Jesus was just another; He was not the one Lord of all. So they came to church on Sunday, but they continued to worship the other deities in their repertoire throughout the week—in secret.

Until one day, when a very bizarre thing happened that changed everything.

Some Jewish high priest's sons were trying to cast out demons from a man; they commanded them to leave in the name of Jesus, whom Paul preached. A demon responded, "Jesus I know, and I know about Paul, but who are you?" (Acts 19:15) Then the demonized man overpowered these seven sons of Sceva, and they were beaten, bloodied, and ran away naked and battered. You have to picture this scene in your mind. Unless you don't have a sense of humor, this is funny! But Luke didn't tell us the story simply because it is humorous; this event produced an amazing outcome. First, the Gentiles were seized with fear and the name of the Lord was held in high honor (Acts 19:17). This story made Jesus famous among the Greeks.

The second result was the church got serious about holiness; they repented of their syncretistic practices. "Many of those who believed now came and openly confessed what they had done. A number who had practiced sorcery brought their scrolls together and burned them publicly. When they calculated the value of the scrolls, the total came to fifty thousand drachmas. In this way the word of the Lord spread widely and grew in power" (Acts 19:18-20). A drachma was a day's wage. In the town where I live in New York, this would translate to about $12 million to $15 million. Fathom that. They were practicing dark magic arts and worshiping other deities to the tune of $12 million to $15 million worth of magic scrolls! They burned $12-15 million worth of magic scrolls! That's a lot of magic, that's a lot of darkness, that's a lot of secret sin. But that day when they heard the story about the seven sons of Sceva, they realized that Jesus wasn't just one of many deities—even the other deities recognized the authority of Jesus.

The church in Ephesus recognized that Jesus was truly Lord, Lord of all other deities, and they decided to stop adding Jesus to their plethora of deities and go all in, exclusively for Jesus.

That day changed the church. The church got serious about fidelity and purity. As a result their lives were dramatically changed and the message of Jesus spread like wildfire. Acts 19:20 reveals the result: "In this way the word of the Lord spread widely and grew in power." The next scene in Acts 19 is a convention—held by the idol-makers. They got together because they felt the conversion and purification rate of the church was a threat to their idol-making income. Listen: When the idol-makers of your community feel economically threatened by the growth and purification rate of the church in your region, that's an authentic move of God! I think this is the greatest move of God that we see among the New Testament churches—it was a significant awakening in a church that impacted the community dramatically.

> Paul attempts to root them in their identity so they will act in authority and realize they have nothing to fear.

Paul ends up writing a letter to this church, and the letter is written to root them in their identity in Christ. After making this decision to leave behind these other deities, the people of Ephesus are afraid. They are fearful of the demonic kickback that will come from their decision to make Jesus their exclusive Lord. They experienced the power of these demonic hosts and were afraid of being the object of their wrath. Paul knew they were afraid, and he writes to help them understand who Jesus really is and who they are in Christ. Paul attempts to root them in their identity so they will act in authority and realize they have nothing to fear. He wants them to know that because Jesus is superior to all other deities and they are in Christ, and Christ is in them, they have authority over these demonic hosts.

The first three chapters of the book to the Ephesians are about their identity in Christ. Over and over Paul's major themes are the phrases that they are in Christ, and He in them, in an attempt to hammer the point home. Thirty times in the book Paul uses this phrase—that they are "in Christ"—including eleven times in the first chapter. This divine union is the key to their identity, their authority, and their victory. The last three chapters are about the implications of this newfound identity in Christ. As a result, in other words, this is how you should live.

The Heavenly Realms

There is a phrase that occurs five times in the book that is fundamental to understanding our authority, and I want to examine these five uses. The phrase is *heavenly realms*, and it is a case study in spiritual authority. Let's look at each use of the phrase in Ephesians.

In Ephesians 1:3, Paul writes, "Praise be to the God and Father of our Lord Jesus Christ, who has blessed us in the *heavenly realms* with every spiritual blessing that is in Christ." He then goes on to list our blessings. For example: He chose us, adopted us, in love predestined us for sonship, redeemed us, forgave us, and sealed us with the Holy Spirit. In 2 Peter 1, Peter tells us that we have everything we need for life and godliness. We have every spiritual blessing we need because we are in Christ, and Christ is in us. We don't need to be afraid of the bullies in the neighborhood because we are part of the family of our all-powerful God. We do not need to be afraid because we have Heaven's storehouse at our disposal; we have everything we need for a triumphant life. Heaven's storehouses are stocked with resources necessary for every victory we need. When we give access to Jesus, we gain access to these storehouses. We must learn how to appropriate Heaven's victories by utilizing the tools of the kingdom of God.

The second time the phrase occurs is later in chapter 1. Paul prays for revelation "that the eyes of your heart may be enlightened" in order that the people of God might know Him—"the hope to which he has called us, the riches of his glorious inheritance . . . and his incomparably great power for us who believe" (Ephesians 1:17-19). Paul prays for revelation, not merely knowledge. Without the revelation of the Holy Spirit we will always live beneath our privileged access. Then he writes, "That power is the same as the mighty strength he exerted when he raised Christ from the dead and seated him at his right hand in the *heavenly realms*, far above all rule and authority, power and dominion, and every name that can be invoked, not only in the present age but also in the one to come. And God placed all things under his feet and appointed him to be head over everything for the church, which is his body, the fullness of him who fills everything in every way" (Ephesians 1:19-22).

Jesus is King and He has no competition for his throne room. The Ephesians had previously worshiped as many as fifty deities, but Jesus isn't like them; Jesus is Lord of all. He is not just another lord among many; He is the Lord of all creation. The Christians in Ephesus didn't need to fear any repercussion from the other deities. There was nothing others could do to overcome the power of Jesus, because He was, and is, their Lord. Who shall we fear? No matter who came against them, or us, no matter what name they came in, no matter what incantation or curse was placed against the Ephesians, or us, they, and we, need not fear because Jesus is Lord. He is supreme. Jesus sits in the heavenly realms far above every other name, every other deity, every other power, every other dominion.

The other deities fear Jesus, so we don't need to fear them; they fear Christ in us. Jesus is never nervous. That alone brings security to our hearts. But Paul doesn't stop there.

The third time the phrase occurs is in Ephesians 2 when Paul says it is by grace we have entered this family of God, not by our own doing, and that we have been delivered from the god of this age who once held us all in captivity, doomed in spiritual death. Ephesians 2:4-6: "But because of his great love for us, God, who is rich in mercy, made us alive with Christ even when we were dead in transgressions—it is by grace you have been saved. And God raised us up with Christ and seated us with him in the *heavenly realms* in Christ Jesus." We are now saved, forgiven, and made alive spiritually by grace. This is important because it means our position cannot be threatened by our own frailty and failings. This is an unmerited position; it is a union of love, not of our doing or making. Therefore, we are secured by the love of this supreme Lord of all.

As amazing as that is, Paul stretches our minds beyond even that: we are seated with Christ in the heavenly realms by grace. We aren't just loved and forgiven, we are given a heavenly seat in the throne room. We have access by grace. Just as Jesus is seated above all powers and rulers and demonic entities, so are we, by grace, seated with Christ in the heavenly realms. Imagine this! He has invited us into rulership with Him; He has given us authority to partner with Him in ruling over the kingdom of darkness. If we could only grasp this picture, it

> If we could only grasp this picture, it would forever change the way we pray. We would pray like Jesus prays because we sit where Jesus sits.

would forever change the way we pray. We would pray like Jesus prays because we sit where Jesus sits. We would battle like Jesus battles because we share in Jesus' reign. We would intercede like Jesus intercedes because we have the access Jesus has. We do not approach God as paupers, we approach Him as princes and princesses: children of the King because of God's rich grace.

It has nothing to do with us. It is by grace that we have been saved, sealed, and seated in the heavenly realms. But it is a terrible loss for the church to live beneath her privileged calling. The world suffers when the church fails to grasp her identity in Christ. When the church fails to act out her privileged position in the heavenly realms, the tyrannical reign of the kingdom of darkness spreads on our planet. If the church could only understand who she is to Jesus, she could touch Heaven and change earth. That's the invitation. Imagine if every time we prayed we took stock of our identity in Christ, our position in Christ, and prayed from that place of the heavenly throne room. What difference would it make in our prayer life? How would it impact our authority?

Paul goes on to mention this phrase a fourth time in Ephesians 3, and this is the most complicated passage to unpack. Let's look at a longer section to catch the context. Ephesians 3:7-12: "I became a servant of this gospel by this gift of God's grace given to me through the working of his power. Although I am less than the least of all the Lord's people, this grace was given to me: to preach to the Gentiles the boundless riches of Christ, and to make plain to everyone the administration of this mystery, which for ages past was kept hidden in God, who created all things. His intent was that now, through the church, the manifold wisdom of God should be made known to the rulers and authorities in the *heavenly realms,* according to his eternal purpose that he accomplished in Christ Jesus our Lord. In him and through faith in him we may approach God with freedom and confidence."

Initially, God created Adam and Eve in His image, and He gave them dominion over the earth—that is, He gave them a kingdom. He gave them the right to rule over their domain, which was earth. They were to rule earth, in His image, in His name, as He ruled heaven. They were to perpetuate His rule and reign on earth. But they rebelled against God. We are spiritual beings in a spiritual world; we are always giving away spiritual access. Remember: we don't get to choose *if* we give away spiritual access, we only get to choose to whom we give away spiritual access. And when Adam and Eve listened to the serpent, they gave spiritual access to the enemy of our souls. Satan became the "god of this age" (2 Corinthians 4:4). His evil kingdom has polluted this planet ever since. But Jesus came. He was the second man, the last Adam (1 Corinthians 15:45). He too was tempted in every way we were, yet without sin (Hebrews 4:15). He gave access only to the Father, and He took back the keys

> Remember: we don't get to choose *if* we give away spiritual access, we only get to choose to whom we give away spiritual access.

of the kingdom that were lost in the fall. He then gave those keys to the church—to redeemed humanity, to their intended owners. He has restored us to our position of rulers and seated us with Him in the heavenly realms so we can pray from our post that His will be done on earth as it is in Heaven. We can touch Heaven and change earth. We become participants in His kingdom initiatives.

Paul is saying here (Ephesians 3) that God did this to display His wisdom to the rulers and powers in the heavenly realms. They thought they had won; they thought we were bound, captive, defeated foes. They thought they had usurped our authority once and for all and now had rulership of the planet. But Jesus came. He turned the tables on the demonic hosts. Now every time a son or daughter prays with authority and enforces God's victory over the minions of hell, God's kingdom invades the earth, His will is done here as it is in Heaven, and the demonic hosts know God's wisdom. Those demons know they have been outsmarted by God; they have been humiliated by His grace to us. God's original plan for humans created in His image to have dominion is fulfilled, and God is magnified for His wisdom in the heavenly realms. The devil's works are destroyed. The prisoners have been set free and have become the cosmic police force to imprison the spirits of darkness and overthrow their dirty deeds. Only God! God gets honor in the cosmos when we understand our authority and rule as we

> It is all by grace, and it is utterly amazing. Therefore, when we fail to act as those who carry privileged access, we rob God of glory.

95

were intended to rule: as image bearers. It is all by grace, and it is utterly amazing. Therefore, when we fail to act as those who carry privileged access, we rob God of glory. If we could only grasp this, we would not need fear the demonic powers, we would not need fear the darkness. Rather, the demonic powers and darkness would fear us because of who we are in Christ.

I notice that sometimes when Christians talk about the demonic realm other Christians get nervous. I've even seen people get fearful. I've seen people get up and leave the room when I am talking about deliverance, or some other similar aspect, because they are so afraid. This always indicates our weak understanding of who Jesus is and who we are in Christ. If we only understood, we would never be afraid. Nor would we be proud; it is only through Christ, by grace, that we are positioned in the rulership of the heavenly realms. We would merely look to Jesus and act in authority for His glory.

The final time the phrase occurs is in Ephesians 6 where Paul explains the reality of the spiritual battlefield. Ephesians 6:10-12: "Finally, be strong in the Lord and in his mighty power. Put on the full armor of God, so that you can take your stand against the devil's schemes. For our struggle is not against flesh and blood, but against the rulers, against the authorities, against the powers of this dark world and against the spiritual forces of evil in the *heavenly realms.*" There is a spir-

> We must pray from our position as sons and daughters, not in fear but in faith. We must pray not against humans, for the true battle is unseen and cosmic in nature.

itual battle taking place around us and, to win, we must take up our seats in the heavenly realms. We must pray from our position as sons and daughters, not in fear but in faith. We must pray not against humans, for the true battle is unseen and cosmic in nature.

Years ago, when I was pastoring, I went through a season of attacks. I felt the Lord calling me to preach on revival, and as I focused on those themes some people started being divisive. I had people blog against me, somebody started a Facebook account with a pseudo name and started posting against me, there were radio shows done against me, and gossip was rampant. In the midst of that I sensed the Lord say to me, "Your battle is not against flesh and blood. These people are not your enemy; they are duped by the enemy." These were all people Jesus loved and for whom He died. I prayed for them, not against them. I blessed them in my prayers, and I prayed against the spiritual forces of darkness that were seeking to damage the work of God. They were duped by the enemy into thinking their battle was against me, but it was not, and neither was my battle against them. Our battle is against the principalities and powers in the heavenly realms. Our battle is to enforce the victories of Jesus over the powers of darkness so Jesus can be glorified.

Every time our kids struggle, our fight as parents is really not against our kids' behaviors, nor is it against our kids' friends; our struggle is in the heavenly realms. Every time politicians make unjust, corrupt decisions, our battle is not against political opponents; our real battle is in the heavenly realms where the prince of this air seeks to rule with injustice. When we battle against racial injustice or gender bias our real battle is in the heavenly realms against forces of darkness that seek to oppress people. Every time drugs rule in our schools, our real battle is not against the drug lords but against the spiritual forces of evil in the heavenly realms that seek to bring bondage. But we are uniquely positioned to win the battle because of who we are in Christ. I am not saying we should not act on the earthly plain to fight against injustices. But too often we fight on the human level, on the earthly level, on the political level, and we see so little impact because we fail to recognize the spiritual forces beyond our problems. When we pray, too often we pray in fear, from a position of weakness, and not in faith from our position in the heavenly realms. When we pray in fear, and act in anger, but fail to take up our position in the heavenly realms, we influence so little change. The more we know who we are in Christ, the more we will pray with authority against the true enemies of our soul and the more we will enforce the victories of Jesus over the prince of darkness.

The problem in Ephesus was that they were keenly aware of the spiritual battle, and they felt afraid and lived like defeated foes. The problem in today's Western church is that too often we are unaware there is a true spiritual battle in the heavenly realms, and we have no idea we are equipped to win it! We too often are fighting a spiritual war with natural weapons, and we don't realize we are ill equipped for the battle. We too often live in fear, act in fear, and pray in fear, and we have no idea how to touch Heaven and change earth. All of our fear, anger, and political

> The problem in today's Western church is that too often we are unaware there is a true spiritual battle in the heavenly realms, and we have no idea we are equipped to win it!

maneuvering has led to so little change. There are forces of darkness influencing the evil realities of our planet; we need to pray with authority while we act in the fullness of truth and fullness of grace. We have been given massive authority to change outcomes, but we are desperately trying to change the world with human plans and human efforts, remaining unaware that we are fighting a spiritual enemy with spiritual positioning in the heavenly realms giving us conquering potential at our fingertips.

One word of caution: We don't want to focus on the enemy or the battle. We want to focus on Jesus and pray from our position in Christ. We have to recognize that there is a real cosmic battle but not give undue attention to the evil one; we must fix our eyes on our Conquering Hero! In the midst of that season when I was under attack at church, and there was much division in the air, there was a lot of instability and fear. I felt it, and so did the rest of our leaders. It felt like everything we had fought for was in jeopardy, like all the ground we had gained was in danger of being lost.

My wife had a dream one night in the middle of that dark season that was incredibly prophetic and instructive. In the dream a group of leaders were at the church property gathered around a bonfire. All of these little demons were running around starting fires around the property, and the leaders began to move all over the grounds to stamp out the little fires the demons had started. A voice came out of the bonfire and said, "In fighting the fires, you forfeit the Flame." The Lord's point was clear: Don't focus on the work of the enemy, focus on the presence of God. Pursue the flame of His presence, not the fires of the enemy.

Strengthening Our identity

How do we strengthen our identity and develop our authority to fight the battle we were called to fight? Paul has some more wisdom to offer in Romans. There are two passages in particular I want to look at and expand upon so we can strengthen our identity and expand our authority—Romans 12 and Romans 8. But first, let's take a look at how our pain and lies form the self-life within us; this often prevents us from living out our identity in Christ. Therefore, these things must be addressed if we are going to step into our true identity in Christ.

If we are going to expand our authority, we must intentionally root ourselves in our identity in Christ. We cannot be passive about it; we must intentionally grow deep roots. Paul wrote in Romans 12:2, "Do not conform to the pattern of this world but be transformed by the renewing of your mind."

We have to rewrite the narrative of our lives if we are going to root ourselves in our identity in Christ.

Identifying the Lies We Believe

Your self-life is most strongly formed in your place of greatest wounding. The place where you were hurt the most growing up is the place where you fortify the strongest. You don't have the ability to process the pain you experience as a child, so you build emotional walls to protect yourself. This deep wounding is where we learn to become self-reliant, self-dependent, self-sufficient, self-centered, and self-pitying. Our most painful wounding in our young life is where our self-life gets entrenched, and until the self-life gets uprooted our identity in Christ is underdeveloped. God, in his mercy, often brings about similar pain in our later years to give us an opportunity to die to self in the very place where self was formed so the Christ life can be formed in us. This is a critically important process in our identity formation.

Let me give an example of how this works. My most significant wounding is around the fear of not being loved. It formed the lie in me that my value was dependent upon whether I could get certain people to love me. I was frequently wounded by unrequited love. It began in me with the childhood wound of separation anxiety and was reinforced along the way many times. There was some bullying, shaming, and rejection that reinforced this wounding. This was the place where my self-life was most strongly formed. I fortified around this wound to protect myself. I had all sorts of shields and self-protective measures built up around this wound. We build these protective measures when we are young, and they become more sophisticated as we age. These walls of self-protection become barriers to intimacy with God and others.

In my own life, the walls of self-protection became most clear in my marriage. For example, if Jen disagreed with me, I would use emotional power in my arguments to persuade her that I was right. I felt threatened by her disagreement, that somehow if she disagreed with me it was because she didn't like me. The unrequited love wound was kicking in, and I used power to try to convince her to agree so she would have to like me. Of course, it didn't work. The forcefulness of my opinions drove her

> The self-life that was formed in my wounding was wounding others around me. It needed to die for the Christ life in me to be formed and my identity strengthened.

away and made her like me less. The self-life that was formed in my wounding was wounding others around me. It needed to die for the Christ life in me to be formed and my identity strengthened.

As I continued to live out of my self-life that was formed in my early wounding, Jen got more hurt and we grew more distant. She finally got to the place where she really didn't like me anymore. This was unrequited love at its very worst—and the pain was so great in my soul it was like a divine scalpel cutting away the cancer of self. It forced me to see things about myself that were broken, sinful, and dysfunctional, areas that needed God's redeeming work. My desperation and eventual cooperation with the Spirit brought me into confrontation with my most significant wounding. It was a divine opportunity—God was giving me an opportunity to come into contact with my wounding so it could be healed. But for that to happen, I had to die to the self-life that was formed from my original wounding to protect my pain. Death to self is painful.

One of my favorite books is Francois Fenelon's *Let Go*. Fenelon says that death to self is painful because it touches that part of us that is most alive; if we were dead already, it wouldn't hurt when God took the scalpel to it. "Our own hands would never put the knife in the right place. We would cut away only a little of the fat and bring about a few superficial changes. . . . And even if we knew where the spot was located, self-love would hold back the knife and spare itself. . . . But the hand of God strikes in unexpected places, finds the very place where the infection is fastened and does not hesitate to cut it away, regardless of the pain. And oh, how self-love cries out! Well, let it cry, but do not let it interfere with the success of the operation" (*Let Go*, Letter 40).[5]

Jesus said, "Whoever wants to be my disciple must deny themselves and take up their cross and follow me. For whoever wants to save their life will lose it, but whoever loses their life for me will find it" (Matthew 16:24, 25). We have to die to the self-life to gain the true life in Christ. The context of this passage is about spiritual authority; Jesus talks to Peter about the keys to the kingdom, about binding and loosing. But we cannot operate in kingdom authority when we are ruled by self. If self rules, Christ doesn't. If self rules, we operate in power and control, not in authority. If we are going to operate in kingdom authority, we must die to self and be ruled by Christ. Then we move from human power to spiritual authority.

There is no freedom in holding on to your self-life. Where self has been formed through wounding, authority is thwarted by our false identity. Until we die to self and give God access to heal the wounding, we cannot stand on the firm foundation of who we are in Christ, and our authority cannot be thoroughly developed. In those early years, my self-life kept moving me to act in power instead of authority. When you act in power, you forgo authority. When you act on your self-life, you reinforce the lies of your soul. We must replace the lies of our damaged souls with the truth of who we are in Christ if we are going to be people of authority and not people who opt for human power displays to control outcomes. And this means we must die to self. I have read Fenelon's *Let Go* more than any other book than the Bible. I have read it so much because I have battled with dying to my self-life. I have discovered that the only time I am truly free is when I die to self, and the only time I am miserable is when my self-life is alive and well. Jesus knows this. Pain and death to self are a divine invitation to identity formation that can lead you to be a person of true spiritual authority.

Some of you won't act in power, you will act in fear. Your wounding has left you feeling powerless, but that is equally a lie that is keeping you from your true identity in Christ. You may have been victimized but you are not a victim, not in Christ you aren't. But as long as you see yourself as a victim through the lens of your wounding, you will continue to forfeit your identity and authority in Christ. Once again, the self-life must die in order for the Christ-life to emerge.

Your identity is like the foundation of a house. No matter how good the builder, no matter how good the building material, if the foundation is not set properly and securely, the house is in jeopardy. And if the house is built on a shaky foundation, cracks are bound to show up. If a life is built on a shaky foundation of wounding and lies, you are sure to have cracks in your soul, and your authority will be greatly diminished. For me, the cracks began showing up in my marriage, but they were a divine invitation to deal with the lies and wounding that were at the heart of my self-life.

Overcoming the Lies We Believe

In my book *Soul Care,* I talk about the three major lies that afflict us.

First, *the people-pleasing lie*: the issue of my value is dependent upon whether certain people love me. For some of us, we don't need every person to like us—just *almost* every person. For others, it is just certain people: people in positions of authority or, say, family members. The reality is that I want Jen to love me; life is better when Jen loves me. But even if Jen doesn't love me, I am going to be OK because Jesus loves me and that is enough. The issue of my value is not dependent on whether Jen loves me, or anyone else for that matter. I knew that cognitively, but I was not living out of that truth. I was living out of the lie, and my self-life was preserving the lie and the hurt beneath.

Second, *the performance lie*: the issue of my value is dependent upon my performance. It may be about moral performance; I feel good about myself as long as I am doing all the things I am supposed to be doing: reading my Bible, praying, going to church, serving, those types of things. And as long as I am not doing all the things I am not supposed to be doing—lusting, getting angry, envious, you know, the whole list of sins. But the reality is that Jesus loved us while we were yet sinners (Romans 5:8). You didn't need to perform to be loved. If you feel like you need to pray long wordy prayers and crawl across glass to get back to God every time you trip up over a besetting sin pattern, you are acting out of the performance lie; that is works righteousness. The issue of your value isn't dependent upon your performance.

Third, *the control lie*: the issue of my value is dependent upon whether I can remain in control. Listen: If anyone ever told you that you are controlling, that's because you *are*. It doesn't do any good to defend yourself. Just own it. Humility begins with honesty and ends with responsibility. We can't change without humility. All three lies have impacted my life.

> Humility begins with honesty and ends with responsibility. We can't change without humility.

By personality, my biggest lie is control. I don't struggle much with wanting to control people; it is much more about controlling outcomes and results. When I can't control these, I feel angry.

By wounding, however, my biggest lie is the people-pleasing one. Wounding left me with the fear of not being loved. And for my identity to get strengthened in Christ, God had to address the lies that were robbing me of who I was.

Rewriting the Narrative of Our Lives

Our story has impacted what we believe about ourselves, and what we believe about ourselves impacts everything we think and do and feel. If we entertain thoughts about ourselves that God does not entertain, we will always live beneath our privilege. Renewing our mind is about rewriting the narrative of our life with the gospel at the center of our story. It is about bringing our thinking into alignment with God's thinking about us and then living like a deeply loved child of God.

If you grew up in a home where you were abused, you have a narrative that runs through your head, and your self-life was formed most strongly around that abuse. Your narrative may sound something like this: "My parents didn't love me; how will anyone else love me? There must be something wrong with me. I'm not lovable; I'm broken. I'm damaged; I'm irreparable." You may even think: *If I could be perfect, then maybe people would love me.* Of course, Jesus was perfect, and they crucified Him, so being perfect won't make you loved. How does your self-life show up? How do you act out on it? Are you defensive? Do you inappropriately power up when you are emotionally threatened? You will have to die to your self-life for the wounds to be healed and your foundation in Christ firmed up.

If you were bullied, you may have a narrative that runs like this: "I am a victim. I feel powerless. There is nothing I can do about this situation. There is no way I can help myself; I can't change my circumstances. I can't change myself." But this is not true. If it is not true about Christ, then it is not true about you in Christ. You have to rewrite the narrative that goes on in your head. You have to rewrite the script of your life with the gospel at the center. How do you act out of your self-life that was formed in bullying? Do you act powerless? How do you feel? Do you feel and act like a victim? Do you feel weak and overwhelmed and behave too passively? Be honest and die to the self-life that was formed in your wounding. In dying, you will live, and your identity will be deepened in Christ and your authority grow.

Three Key Questions

To renew your mind, you have to know when you are standing on the false platform of a lie. You cannot overcome that which you will not admit. Here are the three key questions to ask yourself so you can quickly identify when you are standing on the shaky platform of a lie. When you suspect you're on that false platform, ask:

- What do I think?
- What do I feel?
- How do I act?

If you were bullied and you wrestle with the victim lie, what do you think when you are standing on that platform? What runs through your head unfiltered when you are standing on the lie of the victim? What are the phrases that run through your head? What do you say to yourself about yourself? What are the imaginary conversations you have with other people in your mind? *That which runs through your head unfiltered reveals what is in your heart undealt with*. If you will monitor your self-talk, it will give you clues to your lies and wounds and the place where you must die to self. You may say to yourself, "I can't . . . I can't do this. I can't change that. I can't help this. I can't fix that. I can't overcome this circumstance. *I can't*." What do you feel when you are standing on the lie of the victim? You may feel powerless. You may feel weak, helpless, depressed, fearful, or anxious. You may feel like others are out to get you. You could feel angry, and that gives you a sense of power, and you may feel a desire to exert power in controlling ways. How do you act when you are standing on that lie? You may retreat and isolate. You may get angry and lash out or push people away with power displays.

Knowing how you think, how you feel, and how you act heightens your self-awareness. Self-awareness is the gateway to transformation; it doesn't guarantee it, but you can't get there without it. This is when you need to die to your self-life that has been fortified in wounding and renew your mind: you need to start by knowing when you are standing on the wrong platform, when you are acting on the lies you believe. With God's help, we have to change the lies that have been formed in us through our life experiences. As long as you believe lies about yourself, you will act on them, and they will become a limitation in your interaction with God and others.

Holding on to the Truth

One of Jesus' most famous statements is in John 8:31, 32. We often only quote part of the verse: "You will know the truth, and the truth will set you free." But that isn't what Jesus said. Jesus said, in its full context, "*If* you hold to my teaching, you are really my disciples. Then you will know the truth, and the truth will set you free." It is an *if/then* promise. If you *hold* to his teaching, then you will know the truth, and the truth will set you free. Knowing the teaching of Jesus doesn't, of itself, free us, and that isn't what Jesus taught. Holding to the teaching of Jesus and resetting the narrative of the soul is what sets us free. We have to hold to the truth at precisely the moment the lie is vying for position at the center of our soul.

This means we must let go of our self-life and hold to who we are in Christ. We must die so we can live. We have to hold to the truth when we start to tell ourselves "I can't—because I have been victimized." The truth, instead, is this: "I have been victimized, but I am not a victim. I am more than a conqueror in Christ. I have everything I need for life and godliness." You must hold to that truth until the lie no longer dictates how you think, feel, and act.

Let me give an example of how this works in real time. In the early years of our marriage, when we hit that tough place, the narrative of my soul included the people-pleasing lie. The issue of my value was dependent upon whether I could get certain people to love me, especially Jen. So when Jen didn't love me anymore, I was thrown into a battle with anxiety and fear. It was hitting that old wound of unrequited love. The more I was afraid, the more I tried to make Jen like me. I tried to fix the marriage, fix Jen, fix the problem. I tried to use emotional power to convince her, persuade her, and win her to my side. I was driven by fear. I didn't even know it was fear at the time, but my mind was racing, my chest tightened, I ran through worst-case scenarios in my mind, I was plagued with imaginary conversations with her. Fear was ruling my mind and heart because I wasn't standing on my true identity in Christ. I was standing on a lie: The issue of my value was dependent upon whether I could get Jen to love me. I felt I had to get her to love me to feel good about myself again, to live in peace.

It was the identity lie, in part, that had gotten us into trouble in our marriage. When Jen disagreed with me, I felt threatened and would become more forceful with my opinions; Jen felt as though her opinions were stomped on. My prior wounding was causing me to act out of my self-life, and she was hurt because of how I was acting off of this lie. The more she felt stomped on, the less she liked me, and the more fearful I became. My actions were fearful actions; my prayers were fear-based prayers. I was trying to control and fix the outcomes of my marriage with fear as my fuel because of the lie of my life.

But there is no power in living a lie. There is no freedom in holding on to a lie. There is no peace as long as the lie is the platform you are standing on. You cannot use the tools of the kingdom of darkness to gain freedom in the kingdom of light. You have to hold on to the truth and rewrite the narrative of your life; you must use the tools of the kingdom of light to gain access to the victories of Jesus. The narrative that ran through my head was fear-based. I had to rewrite the script. I wasn't living out the truth. I had to hold on to the truth and live out of it.

Victory starts with self-awareness. I had to recognize the narrative that was running through my head. You can't change

> There is no peace as long as the lie is the platform you are standing on. You cannot use the tools of the kingdom of darkness to gain freedom in the kingdom of light. You have to hold on to the truth and rewrite the narrative of your life.

that which you won't admit, and you can't get free from that which you do not recognize. Self-awareness was the gateway to life change; I had to see the truth about myself. When I was standing on this false platform of the fear of not being loved, what was I thinking? What did I feel? How did I act?

Whenever I stepped out onto that unstable, fearful platform my thinking sped up. My mind started racing; I couldn't shut it down. I would go over the situation in my mind again and again. I would obsess about the problems and worst-case scenarios. I would be driving down the road and find myself engaged in an imaginary conversation with Jen—and these kinds of things kept coming to the surface because fear was fueling my thinking as I stood on a lie. When we actually talked, she would tell me the things she was upset about, and I would defend myself, justify myself. I would show her where she was wrong. Insecure people cannot take ownership; they defend themselves and blame others. Only secure people admit the truth about themselves. Insecure people are defensive; secure people take responsibility. I wasn't yet secure enough in Christ to simply own my part. I knew the truth of the gospel, but it hadn't permeated my heart in such a way that it changed my actions in my relationship with Jen. And every time I had this imaginary conversation in my head, and every time I defended myself in a real conversation with her, what I was doing was reinforcing the lie. When you act on the lie, you give power to the lie.

What did I feel? I felt the effects of fear. I felt defensive. I felt angry. I felt hurt. I felt anxiety. Those were my clues that I had wandered off the platform of the truth that I am deeply loved by God—again, I was standing on the lie.

How did I act? I acted in ways inconsistent with Jesus. I acted on my self-life; all of my self-protective walls came up around my wounded heart. When I was hurt in marriage, I withdrew. I would wall up, numb out, become silent, disengage emotionally, and engage in self-centered behavior. When I was challenged and felt threatened, I powered up emotionally in self-protective ways. I acted with power—my opinions stomped Jen's opinions because I was afraid if she disagreed she wouldn't like me. These actions—withdrawal, silence, anger, defensiveness—became the real clues that I was standing on a lie. I had to get back to the truth. As I began to become aware of what I thought, how I felt, and how I acted when I was standing on this false platform, I was one step closer to holding on to the truth and overcoming. I could preach the truth, quote the passages, and declare the truth, but as long as I was living off the lie, the truth was not integrated into my life. Without admitting to myself how the lie was impacting me, and without holding to the truth, I couldn't change.

John said, "If we claim to have fellowship with Him and yet walk in the darkness, we lie and do not live out the truth" (1 John 1:6). My problem wasn't that I didn't "know" the truth. My problem was I wasn't living out the truth. I was living out my self-life, not the Christ life. *When you have a lack of integration of the gospel, you have disintegration in your life.* And I couldn't live it out until I walked in the light with God—I had to allow God to show me how I had not lived out the truth of the gospel. I needed Him to show me how I was living like a man not loved, not as a man who had been chosen before the foundations of the earth and was deeply loved by the Father in Heaven.

James wrote that "faith by itself, if it is not accompanied by action, is dead" (2:17). Faith without deeds is dead. When I acted like an unloved person, my faith in the gospel was dead to me because I wasn't living it out. It was cognitive but not transformative. It was mental agreement but not life alignment. It was information but not assimilation of the truth. I had a mental assent to the truths of the gospel, but they had not been integrated into my life. They weren't impacting the way I was living in my marriage.

That was not because of the impotence of the truth, nor because of the power of the lie. I hadn't learned how to hold on to the truth in a way that rewrote the storyline of my life. I hadn't rescripted my life with the gospel at the center. I had to hold to the truth; simply knowing the truth does not change us, and that is not what Jesus taught. I knew God loved me; I could have told you God loved me. I preached that God loved you and me. But again, I was living off of the lie. We must hold to the truth precisely when the lie is disrupting our lives. This is why we have to recognize what the lie looks like in our daily existence.

This is what I started telling myself when I realized I was standing on the lie: "I want Jen to like me. Life is better when Jen likes me. But even if Jen doesn't like me, I am going to be OK because Jesus loves me and that is enough for me. The issue of my value was settled at the cross. On the cross of Christ, the Father declared He loved me so much that I was worthy of His Son's blood." *Those things* are the truth. I started telling myself that every time I felt afraid, defensive, like withdrawing, hurt, anxious, and every time I started having an imaginary conversation with Jen. Imaginary conversations became illegal for me! The only reason I had the imaginary conversations was because the lie was so compelling. Faith without deeds is dead. We cannot live in peace when we hold on to a lie.

The more you know how you think, how you feel, and how you act when you are standing on a lie, the quicker you can identify the false platform and begin to shift to the truth. Then you must tell yourself the truth; you must hold to the truth. But it can't just stop with declarations. I hear lots of people trying to hold to the truth by making truth declarations to themselves, but they are doing it in fear and then they act out the lies of their soul anyway; their declarations don't help them at all. If you pray in fear, it reinforces your fear. You have to shift from fear to faith. If you declare in fear, it reinforces your fear. Let the Holy Spirit minister the truth to your heart, mind, and soul. Then act on the truth! If it hasn't changed the way you act, then you haven't held to the truth. It's merely a cognitive belief, not a deeply held, lived-out conviction.

Living It Out

When Jen and I were struggling, this is the process I went through. Every night I would ask her what she was upset about, and she would tell me. In the beginning, I was defensive, angry, hurt, sullen, and fearful. She would feel hurt that I wasn't listening, and we were getting nowhere. One night I was alone with God and He said to me, "Don't defend yourself again." I said, "But Lord, defensiveness is one of my best tools." He said, "Every time you defend yourself you are deflecting the light that I offer to help you. Stop defending yourself and listen." So I decided I was going to go into these conversations and not defend myself. I still felt defensive, but I chose not to act on it. I was dying to self.

This was the first step in letting down the walls of the self-life and giving God access to my wounded heart. I would listen, seek to understand, and then get alone with God and process with Him before I responded to Jen. After the conversation, in my time alone with God, I would secure my identity in Christ. I held on to the truth; I reminded myself that I was deeply loved: "I want Jen to like me. Life is better when Jen likes me. But even if Jen doesn't like me, I'm going to be OK because Jesus loves me and that's enough for me. The issue of my value is settled at the cross." After I told myself the truth, I would sit and listen for the Holy Spirit to remind me of the gospel truths that I am deeply loved. I quieted my soul and listened for the Spirit's voice. I was rooting my identity in Christ. You can't simply do it with declaration; you need revelation.

> I quieted my soul and listened for the Spirit's voice. I was rooting my identity in Christ. You can't simply do it with declaration; you need revelation.

After I solidified my position in Christ by holding on to the truth and listening for His revelation, I asked the Lord, "Of these things Jen talked to me about today, what is true?" I could hear the truth from God when I was secure in love. Insecure people cannot receive the truth even though it is a gift to them. Insecure people have to prop themselves up with lies because they aren't holding to the truth of God about themselves. We have to get on our secure foundation as deeply loved people in order to see the truth about ourselves and own it. But when we do, we know we are deeply loved. Insecure people blame—they blame God, they blame others, they even blame themselves in self-hating, self-incriminating ways that leave them feeling powerless to change.

Insecure people don't own things; they don't take responsibility for their part and move forward with a plan to change. Only secure people own their part, take responsibility, and move forward with hope to change. They exercise their will and authority. After securing my foundation, and owning my part before the Lord, I was ready for action. Finally, I would say to myself, "Now, how would a deeply loved, secure person, chosen from the foundations of the earth, act right now?" I didn't always feel like a deeply loved person, *but this was true whether I felt like it or not.* Faith is about stepping out in obedience whether we feel the reality of the truth we believe or not. I determined to live out the new life that was mine in Christ; I chose to live like a deeply loved person. Remember what James said: faith without deeds is dead. I determined to live out of the firm foundation of God's love, and that required obedient acts of faith. I had to die to self and live the life Jesus wanted. Unless we act on the truth, we don't own the truth, and we don't integrate the truth into our lives. We must act on the truth to take the roots of our identity deep.

After doing this thousands of times, my roots were sinking deep. I used to live on the shaky foundation and occasionally visit the true foundation. But now I live on the true foundation and only occasionally visit the false one. I've shifted my abode. That is the power of renewing the mind.

The Revelation of the Spirit

Second, not only must we intentionally root ourselves in our identity by holding on to the truth and renewing our mind, we must put ourselves in the place to receive the revelation of the Holy Spirit. I briefly mentioned this in my marriage story, how I would listen for the Holy Spirit to reveal the love of God to me. *The gap in most of our Christian lives is the gap between what we know and what has not yet been made known to us by the Holy Spirit.* Knowledge is informational, but revelation is transformational. We need revelation to live out our Christian life. When you are not experiencing the revelatory love of the Father, your intimacy with God will be stunted and your authority in Christ underdeveloped. But we must create space for God to reveal the truths of our identity to us. We must create a still place in our soul where we listen to the voice of God.

> The gap in most of our Christian lives is the gap between what we know and what has not yet been made known to us by the Holy Spirit.

In Romans chapter 8, Paul talks about life in the Spirit. He explains to us that we are no longer controlled by the sinful nature, but instead we have victory because the Spirit of Christ now lives in us. We are in Christ and Christ is in us—we have the victory of Jesus at our disposal. He goes on to say, in verses 14 through 17: "For those who are led by the Spirit of God are the children of God. The Spirit you received does not make you slaves, so that you live in fear again; rather, the Spirit you received brought about your adoption to sonship. And by him we cry, 'Abba, Father.' The Spirit himself testifies with our spirit that we are God's children. Now if we are children, then we are heirs—heirs of God and co-heirs with Christ, if indeed we share in his sufferings in order that we may also share in his glory."

The Spirit does not want us to live in fear. When we act on fear, we are acting in a manner inconsistent with a deeply loved child of God because perfect love drives out fear (1 John 4:18). Fear always robs us of our authority and often moves leaders to operate from a need to control. Fear is a tool of the enemy to keep you from the freedom and fullness of God. Fear makes it too much about us: when we are afraid we get our eyes on ourselves and make it about our abilities, our resources, our capacity, and our competency. Fear fuels the self-life. Faith gets our eyes off ourselves and onto God. The Spirit reveals who we are in Christ, so we no longer need to operate out of fear; we can operate out of faith.

> Fear makes it too much about us: when we are afraid we get our eyes on ourselves and make it about our abilities, our resources, our capacity, and our competency.

We do not need to fear messing up—we are accepted, and deeply loved—while we are yet sinners (Romans 5). We do not need to fear being inadequate; we have the same Spirit in us that was in Christ. We have a High Priest who pleads our cause. We don't have what it takes by ourselves, but we have what it takes, in Christ, to touch Heaven and change earth. We don't have to fear rejection; we have been accepted like we are God's own Son. We don't have to fear failure; Jesus' righteousness was credited to us and we already have approval of the

Father. We don't have to fear abandonment; we are welcomed into an eternal home where we forever belong, and we already have the deposit of His Spirit within us. We don't have to fear demons or Satan or hell; we are united with the King of kings who is Lord of lords. We don't have to fear hardship or suffering; God can redeem everything that comes into our lives to make us more like Jesus (Romans 8:28-39). We don't have to fear death; Jesus has overcome death and conquered the grave. We don't have to fear anything, because Christ is in us and Jesus isn't nervous. He is the unchallenged King.

Paul goes on to write to the church at Rome, "Who shall separate us from the love of Christ? Shall trouble or hardship or persecution or famine or nakedness or danger or sword? . . . No, in all these things we are more than conquerors through him who loved us. I am convinced that neither death nor life, neither angels nor demons, neither the present nor the future, nor any powers, neither height nor depth, nor anything else in all creation, will be able to separate us from the love of God that is in Christ Jesus our Lord" (Romans 8:35-39). Exactly! John wrote that perfect love drives out fear. When we root ourselves deeply in the love of God and listen for the Spirit's revelation that we are deeply loved children, we can begin to move in faith, not fear, and act in authority.

The Spirit brought about our adoption to sonship—this is a technical term used by Paul that refers to firstborn son status. It's a fact that the firstborn son had special status in this society. In order to keep the family wealth, which was mostly in land and livestock, the firstborn got most of the inheritance. In this case, the firstborn in the family of God is Jesus. What is Paul saying? That we have firstborn status! Really? Hang on.

The Spirit in us cries "Abba, Father." That is the exact way Jesus addressed His Father when He walked the earth; we are given the same address because the same Spirit that lived in Jesus lives in us. We are loved like Jesus. We are adopted through Jesus. We belong. We are family. We have firstborn status. But there is still more proof of this.

Paul goes on to say that "the Spirit himself testifies with our spirit that we are God's children" (Romans 8:16). The Spirit is revealing that we are God's children. Think about a testimony, a witness. If you were walking down the street today and you saw an accident, you would be a witness. A witness tells what they have seen, what they heard, and what they experienced. Paul says the Spirit testifies, witnesses to our spirit, that we are children of God! The Spirit testifies to what He has seen, what He has heard, and what He has experienced in the heavenly realms. If you are a Christian, He testifies to what He has heard the Father say about you—that you belong to Him, that you are His son, His daughter. The Spirit testifies to what He has experienced in Heaven; He has experienced the power of Jesus' blood to purify you from all your sin. Nothing is held against you; the enemy's accusations cannot stick because of the efficacy of the blood of Christ.

> The problem is we often discredit the witness of the Spirit because of the garbage we carry in the suitcase of our souls.

The Spirit knows this and He is witnessing to you about it. He has heard the enemy bring accusations against you that did not stick because of Christ's blood shed for you and Christ's righteousness in you. The problem is we often discredit the witness of the Spirit because of the garbage we carry in the suitcase of our souls. The enemy knows what we have done, and so do we. When he brings it up and throws it in our face, we often allow his accusations and our identity lies to deflect the witness of the Spirit. The lies we believe and the wounds we carry often keep us from trusting the Spirit's witness. The Spirit witnesses to us that we are deeply loved, but we tell ourselves, "If my father abandoned me, how can I be loved by God? There must be something wrong with me. I'm not lovable." And the narrative of our story often causes us to discredit the witness of the Spirit. This is why we must unpack the suitcase of our soul; this is why we must die to self and give Jesus access to our wounds. We have to identify these lies and break them. We must still our souls and listen to the testimony of the Spirit without discrediting the revelation He brings.

Part of the process of breaking free from the lies is to listen to the Spirit's testimony about the Father's love for us. So how do we experience the testimony, the witness of the Spirit? How do we receive the revelation we need that can sink our roots deep and help us develop authority? Let me give you three ways to receive the Spirit's testimony. But before I do, let's take a minute to talk about how to prepare your heart to hear.

I have to cultivate stillness in order to prepare my heart to receive revelation. When I am trying to still my heart, I pray out all the things that are going to distract me. I make sure my confessions are current; I ask the Lord to bring up anything I need to confess, and I bring it to Jesus. I also pray through things that are

> I have to cultivate stillness in order to prepare my heart to receive revelation. When I am trying to still my heart, I pray out all the things that are going to distract me.

troubling to me. I pray through any kid troubles, marriage troubles, financial troubles, work troubles, or current world problems like the pandemic of COVID-19. Whatever it is that may rob me of peace and stillness, I pray through until I can surrender it and leave it with God. I also pray through my to-do list. If I don't pray about it, it will distract me when I go to listen to the Spirit. After I have talked through all of these potential distractions, I meditate on a passage of Scripture or sing some worship songs to move my focus onto God. I cultivate a sense of God's presence, and now my soul is still and I'm ready to receive the revelation of the Spirit.

Three Ways to Receive from the Spirit

Once you have prepared your heart for stillness, there are three ways to receive the Spirit's revelation.

First, we receive the Spirit's testimony of the adoptive love of the Father when the Spirit illuminates Scripture to us. 2 Timothy 3:16 says, "All Scripture is God-breathed and is useful for teaching, rebuking, correcting and training in righteousness." All Scripture is God-breathed. Now, most of the time when preachers explain this passage, they say it means that the Holy Spirit superintended the process of writing the Scriptures so that the Word is inspired and infallible. I believe that to be true. But I am not convinced that's exactly what Paul meant when he wrote these words. I think what Paul meant was this: Every time you pick up this holy writ called

Every time you pick up this holy writ called Scripture, you are one Holy Spirit breath away from a fresh encounter with the living God.

Scripture, you are one Holy Spirit breath away from a fresh encounter with the living God. Every time you read the Bible, the Spirit can breathe on a passage and stir something deep within you, and you can encounter God. We must put ourselves in a place of receiving the revelation of the Spirit—especially when it comes to taking our identity deep.

One day I realized that I needed to expand my authority and that it was rooted in identity, so I started meditating on Scripture connected to my identity. I had done this early in my marriage struggle too, but this was a few years later, and I was trying to take it deeper. I was meditating on this passage in Romans 8 and I felt the Spirit stirring me at verse 17: "Now if we are children, then we are heirs—heirs of God and co-heirs with Christ, if indeed we share in his sufferings in order that we may also share in his glory." We must be willing to share in His sufferings because He is the God of the cross. When Jesus calls you to follow Him, He calls you to pick up your cross. Only to the degree to which we are willing to suffer with Him and die to self can we move in authority. But the phrase that jumped out at me that day, the phrase where I felt the breath of the Spirit, was "heirs of God and co-heirs with Christ." I lingered with it.

I was at the monastery at the time. And it struck me that Paul was saying the things that belong to Jesus belong to us— if we are willing to share in His sufferings. If you are willing to fully identify with Christ, even in His death, then you get access like Christ. We are co-heirs. We have access to the things Jesus has access to. This fits with Paul's thinking in Ephesians. Christ is seated in the heavenly realms, and we are seated with Christ in the heavenly realms. The stuff that belongs to Jesus belongs to us. This is a mind-boggling idea.

As I sat there meditating on this concept my cell phone rang. This was unusual; I never get a signal at the monastery. I looked down and it was my daughter Courtney; she was in high school at the time. I picked up the phone and she said, with an urgent tone, "Dad, can I talk to you?" I spoke quickly. "Courtney, I'm at the monastery. I never get a signal here. I am going to go and call you from the monastery phone. The caller ID will say 'Most Holy Trinity Monastery.' Pick up—it's me, not the monks."

I hung up and went to call her on the monastery phone. We talked for a few minutes, I helped her resolve her problem, and I went back to my room. I started meditating on Romans 8 again—and then it hit me.

If any other name had been on that caller ID, I would have ignored it. I was in my sacred space. No one gets access to my sacred space when I am alone at the monastery. I am there to meet with God. But the name on the phone was Reimer; it was one of my kids. And my kids get access to my sacred space because they carry my name. We are God's children and we carry the family name because of what Jesus has done for us. We get access to the sacred space, the throne room of the Father, because we carry the name of Jesus. We are heirs of God, co-heirs with Christ. We get access because Jesus gets access and we are seated with Christ in the

> We are God's children and we carry the family name because of what Jesus has done for us. We get access to the sacred space, the throne room of the Father, because we carry the name of Jesus.

heavenly realms. We need the revelation of the Spirit to make this known to us so we can begin to live it.

I need the illumination of the Spirit on a regular basis for the roots of my identity to go deep. I spend regular time meditating on passages about my identity in Christ to give the Spirit space to illuminate the Scripture and take those truths deep in my soul. Deep roots cannot happen without the benefit of time. Deep roots do not occur merely with knowledge; there must be the illumination of the Spirit. If you want to expand your authority, you must be rooted in identity. If you want to move mountains, carve out time to meditate on Scriptures that speak to your identity and give the Spirit opportunity to illuminate them and take them deep into your soul. Linger with the Spirit in the Word.

Second, we receive the Spirit's testimony about the adoptive love of the Father through direct revelation. The Spirit testifies, He witnesses, with our spirit. But we have to give Him space to speak. We have to quiet our souls so we can hear that still, small voice.

Early in my spiritual journey I started a prayer journal. On a regular basis I would take time to write down what I sensed the Spirit was saying. Most days I would spend some time quieting my heart, and then I would give space for God to speak. I would sit quietly before the Lord and wait for the Holy Spirit to speak. In John 14-16 Jesus said the Holy Spirit would lead us, guide us, make known to us, reveal to us, teach us, remind us, convict us—these are all communication verbs. God speaks; we need to learn how He speaks to us. Every day as I listened, I wrote down what I sensed the Spirit was saying to me.

Most days the Lord would start by saying, "I love you." I would write it down. He might go on to say other things to me. The next day I would begin listening again, and the Lord would say, "I love you." I'd write it down. This went on for months. One day I said to the Lord, "Is that really your voice? Is that just me? Am I just hearing what I want to hear?" At the time I had a newborn, and I heard the Lord say to me, "Don't you tell your daughter you love her every day?" I said, "Yes, but she is my daughter."

Yup. Sometimes we are a little slow to pick up what God is putting down. Heirs of God. Co-heirs with Christ. Deeply loved.

One day my newborn first child, my daughter, got up in the middle of the night. I got up with her. She finally fell asleep in my arms as we sat and rocked in the dark in our living room. I felt my heart expanding with love. I just let out a low groan in the dark as I whispered, "I love you." And I heard the Spirit whisper deep within me: "That's how the Father feels about you. He loves you—even more." I've been listening to the Spirit's voice for nearly thirty years, and still most days I hear God say, "I love you." The Spirit testifies with our spirit that we are the deeply loved, adopted children of God. We need to hear it to take our roots deep.

I have done thousands of deliverances. At the end of a deliverance the Spirit often speaks directly to the person. Many times they hear God speak for the first time, and the thing He says most often is "I love you." I've seen hundreds of people hear the Spirit's testimony about the Father's love and break down and sob. Life-hardened

Life-hardened men and women who have seldom shed a tear break down and melt under the testimony of the Spirit that they are deeply loved.

men and women who have seldom shed a tear break down and melt under the testimony of the Spirit that they are deeply loved. It is the thing the Spirit of God most often speaks into our inner being (that's precisely what Paul said): that the Spirit testifies with our spirit that we are the deeply loved children of God. The more we believe it, the more we receive it, the more we internalize it, the deeper our roots will go in our identity, and the more we will be able to move mountains.

If you haven't been doing this, why don't you carve out five minutes a day to listen to the Holy Spirit? Quiet your heart and listen to His voice. And don't discredit the testimony of the Spirit. Write it down and receive it.

Third, we receive the Spirit's testimony about the adoptive love of the Father when the Spirit pours out the love of God in our hearts. Romans 5:5: "God's love has been poured out into our hearts through the Holy Spirit, who has been given to us." There are times when the Spirit speaks into our inner being—with a testimony, a still, small voice—and it is like a trickle of love into our hearts. If I had a drippy hose, and I held it over you, eventually I could get you soaked, but it would take a long time. But if I turned that hose on full blast, it wouldn't take long for you to get soaked. If I threw you off a dock into a lake, you would be soaked in even less time.

We need the Spirit to illuminate the Scriptures and we need the quiet whispers of the Spirit's testimony on a regular basis. But it really helps to have an occasional drenching of the Father's love too! We can have encounters with the Spirit that leave us soaked; we can have encounters with the Spirit where the Father's love is poured out in our hearts. And when we have those they can shift something in our authority, and the shift can be quite sudden and notable.

I had an encounter with the Father's love in a dream one day, and it changed me. I have told this story in other books, but not as it relates to spiritual authority. So allow me to tell it here and talk about the impact the experience had on my spiritual authority. I had been in ministry for about ten years when I began to notice something about my walk with God. I connected to two of the three members of the Trinity deeply. I connected deeply with Jesus—I loved Jesus and felt very connected to Jesus. I connected to the Holy Spirit—I sensed His presence, I heard His voice, I felt His love.

But the Father seemed distant to me. I noticed in my prayers that I always addressed Him as "God." I'm not a religious person; I don't use a lot of religious phrases when I pray. I simply pray from the heart, and my prayers were quite revealing to me. I used intimate expressions to speak to Jesus and the Spirit, but not when I addressed the Father. I simply felt distant from Him. I could even sense a little aversion in my soul toward Him, though I didn't know why.

I started praying. "Jesus, I don't know the Father like you know the Father. I don't experience Him like you talk about Him. Show me the Father. Reveal the Father to me." I wasn't passive; I started taking steps to put myself in a position to receive the testimony of the Spirit. I took time each day to meditate on passages of

Scripture. It was during this time that I was meditating on Romans 8 and had that encounter with God at the monastery that I just wrote about. That helped—the hose was filling my barrel. I listened each day for the Spirit's testimony, and I heard His voice regularly and wrote down what I sensed He was saying. It was helping. But I knew there was more! I had read that passage in Romans 5 countless times, and I was praying for an outpouring of the Father's love.

One night I had a dream. Dreams are very symbolic, and the symbolism is significant, but it took me a while to unpack all the symbols in the dream. In the dream I was speaking at a men's retreat with people I did not know. Why a men's retreat? Because, like Moses, I was wrestling with my identity. Moses hid his face from God because of shame. I had been through the marriage crisis already, and I had worked on my identity. I had made huge progress, but I wasn't done yet. John says that when we meet Jesus face to face, we shall become like Him (1 John 3). It takes one day longer than a lifetime to become like Jesus. When we meet Him face to face we'll be like Him; in the meantime we are on a journey. I still had shame that needed to be addressed so I could go deeper in my identity. Shame is like Teflon; nothing sticks to Teflon, and the love of God doesn't stick to our shame. My shame was blocking the Father's love—just as Moses' had.

The dream began at the end of the men's retreat. I was leaving the platform. As I made my way across the floor all of these men were hugging me and saying goodbye. But they were giving me man hugs: three pats and you're out. Anything more than that is definitely suspicious! I made my way across the floor and out the door. There was a man there, outside on the steps, who had been critical of me. But that man didn't represent himself in the dream; as I said, dreams are symbolic. He represented the critic within. When you carry shame, you are often your own worst critic. Shame blames, and in my case, the person it mostly blamed was me. I was driven, demanding much of myself. He was the only man in the dream I didn't hug. That's because you can't make peace with shame, you have to put it to death.

I walked to the parking lot, and there was one last man in the lot. He was about my dad's age at the time of the dream, and he gave me a hug like everyone else. The only problem was: no one taught him the man hug rules! He hugged me uncomfortably close for an uncomfortably long period of time. Everything inside of me wanted to get away from him. My skin was crawling. Finally he released the embrace, looked me in the eye, and said, "I am your Father in Heaven and I love you." And I lost it. I collapsed in His arms and sobbed.

> Finally he released the embrace, looked me in the eye, and said, "I am your Father in Heaven and I love you." And I lost it. I collapsed in His arms and sobbed.

I woke up and my pillow was soaking wet with my tears. I got out of bed and sat in the dark, just drenched in the Father's love. And it changed me.

The Father's Compassion

After that encounter with the Father I started having a new experience. I would walk into a room and feel the Father's compassion for someone. It wasn't my compassion. It wasn't Jesus' compassion. It wasn't the Spirit's compassion. It was uniquely and distinctly the Father's compassion, and I knew what it was because I had experienced it. I would walk up to the person and say, "I feel the Father's compassion for you." And the person would collapse in my arms and weep. It happened dozens of times. People would have breakthroughs as I prayed for them. The new encounter I had with the Father's love poured out in my heart had led to new authority because it had deepened the roots of my identity.

I also started noticing a pattern: I would feel the Father's compassion for people who were in pain even if I didn't know they were in pain! I would sense the Father's compassion and sometimes I would know exactly why—I knew the pain they were carrying in their soul and I could address it with prophetic insight and the person would encounter God. This has happened hundreds of times since that encounter with the Father.

I was in a hotel one day waiting to speak to a group of missionaries. I was having coffee with a friend and I noticed a woman walking across the hotel lobby. I said to my friend, "Do you see that young lady? She was molested by her father." He said, "How do you know that?" "Wait and see," I said. "If she is one of our missionaries at this conference, I will do her deliverance before the week is over. And then I'll tell you how I knew."

A little later we went up to the conference room and, sure enough, the woman was sitting in the room; she was a missionary at our conference. I was speaking in the first session. I wasn't scheduled to teach on deliverance or do any deliverance, but someone raised their hand during my talk and asked, "Will you train us in deliverance?" There was some free space one of the days, so I offered to use the free space to do a training for anyone who wanted to come. I prayed that the woman I saw in the lobby would come. I didn't care who else came, but I wanted her to come, because I knew she needed to get free.

A couple of days later the time for the deliverance training came, and the first person to come into the room was the woman. I walked up to her and said, "I was praying that you would come." She said, "I have been waiting to meet you for years. I have heard about your ministry and I have been anxious to meet you." I could see her desperation. I was very direct. I said, "Can I ask you a question?" She nodded. "Were you sexually abused by your father?" She nodded again. I asked her if she was experiencing sexual attacks in the night from demonic spirits, which is, sadly, an all-too-common experience for people who have been sexually abused. They will wake up in the night and have physical sensations of a sexual encounter—but no one is there. It is a demonic spirit attacking them. It is so dark, so evil, and so torturous. She told me she had been experiencing those demonic attacks regularly for a decade as a missionary.

That day I did her deliverance, and she was free.

My friend was dying to know how I knew she was sexually abused by her father. I experienced the Father's compassion for her, so I knew she was carrying pain. The person may be laughing, and seem to be carefree, but when I feel the Father's compassion, I know they are carrying pain. I will sometimes walk up to a person and say to

When I feel the Father's compassion coupled with the Father's ferocity, I know the person has been sexually abused. It is the only time I have the collision of these two emotions.

them, "You are carrying sadness in your soul. Are you aware of that?" They will start sobbing. But when I feel the Father's compassion coupled with the Father's ferocity, I know the person has been sexually abused. It is the only time I have the collision of these two emotions. That's what I sensed that day, and it came with the knowledge deep in my spirit that her father was the abuser.

That encounter with the Father's love solidified my identity, broke through a wall of my shame, and increased my authority. I immediately started to carry a new level of God's presence into encounters with people and these led to breakthroughs. I was nearly fifteen years into ministry at that time in my life, but after that encounter my spiritual authority immediately expanded, and it was noticeable. This is why we have to keep going after our identity and keep taking it deeper. There is always more. I felt I had conquered my identity issues during my marriage crisis. But there was more. I felt I had expanded my authority greatly with this encounter with the Father's love. And I had. But there was more.

Testing and Authority

I had an encounter years later with the Father's love, one that was far less dramatic and yet even more impactful. It followed a dark night of the soul in which the presence of God was absent from my life for a fairly long and hard season. For many months I had no sense of God's presence and no sense of God's voice. It was a very hard season in my life where promises I had fought for over many years were all stalled in coming forth. I was deeply discouraged.

Still, I kept showing up every day; I waited for God's presence to return. It was a long season of testing, and all I could do was endure and try to keep my heart soft before God. One day as I sat alone with God I sensed that old familiar presence once again. I wept. I wept simply because I had missed Him so much. The encounter was a gentle reentry of the Father's loving presence, but when it returned, my identity was deepened, and my authority was greatly expanded. I continue to pursue God to take my roots deeper and pour out the Father's love more, because God is infinite, and there is always more.

Prior to that dark night of the soul I had prayed for twenty years that God would give me the ability to impart His Spirit—if my character and intimacy were able to sustain it. I had read the book of Acts; I had studied the history of revival and found that, often, movements of God were catapulted with people being filled with the Spirit through the laying on of hands. In other words, there was impartation. And that was what I was praying for, but I prayed it would only be granted if my character and intimacy could sustain it because I did not want to do anything to dishonor Jesus. The dark night was necessary for deepening my intimacy, for my character formation, and for more of the self-life to die so God could fulfill that prayer. And when His presence returned there was a new level of authority, a new level of confidence in God's intervening power. The very next conference I went to, God intervened, and people started getting filled with the Holy Spirit. For a long season after that dark night of the soul ended, most of the people I prayed for to be filled with the Spirit encountered God with power. Spiritual authority is rooted in identity. Identity roots go deep when we encounter the Father's love. It doesn't always look the same, but it is fundamental to the expansion of authority.

In order to be rooted, to be deepened, in identity it is necessary for our identity to be tested. God doesn't test us so we will fail; God tests us so we will pass. Trials are necessary for character development and identity strengthening. When we go through a trial it often feels like we are losing ground, but when we come out the other side we realize we have been strengthened in character and identity. That's what happened to me after that dark night of the soul. We must hold to who we are in Christ, to what God says about us. When darkness invades, never let go of what God has told you in the light. Jesus was tested in his identity: "If you are the Son of God . . . " Moses was tested in his identity; he was tested by the most severe trials, tribulations, and rebellions. The disciples were tested in their identity by persecution and trials.

> When darkness invades, never let go of what God has told you in the light.

Everyone who wants to go deeper must go through the waters of testing without letting go of who they are in Christ. We must go through the necessary struggle of holding to what God has told us about ourselves even when our circumstances seem to the deny the truth we believe. The struggle of holding to the truth strengthens your grip on the truth and allows our identity roots to go deep.

All too often, however, we enter a time of testing and try to pray out the very thing God needs to bring in so we can become the very people we want to become. We are pursuing God for more of Himself, and to expand our authority, and trials come our way. And we start to pray out the trials, but they are the very tools we need to allow our roots to go deep. When we fail to embrace trials, we find ourselves fighting against the work of God in our soul.

Our identity doesn't grow deep roots because we go to church, because we read our Bible, or because we pray. It doesn't happen haphazardly. We have to be intentional. We can't be passive. We have to hold on to the truth. And when you hold on consistently, over time, your roots will sink deep, and this process will change you and expand your authority.

A few years ago, Jen went back to the workplace. My wife is a very bright, incredibly capable woman. She got an entry level job as a part-time secretary in a higher education institution. Within months, however, she was promoted to the head of finances in her area. She was so excited. She started reading a book on networking. One night at bedtime she was telling me about it; she was talking about how the author networked. The whole time she was talking about it I grew irritated, like this was the worst book in the world. I had a little verbal vomit moment about this stupid book, and I walked out of the bathroom into our bedroom. My wife continued to brush her teeth and just became quiet. I went into our bedroom and processed, for about forty-five seconds, what had just happened. I walked back into the bathroom and said, "Let me explain what just happened. You are back in the workplace, and you are an incredibly bright, beautiful, winsome person. I am traveling quite a bit these days. I am afraid that someone will come and sweep you off your feet and I will lose you. That's just the junk in the suitcase of my soul. That's just my fear of not being loved. You keep networking, and I'll deal with my junk and we will be fine."

She looked at me in surprise and said, "You unpacked that in forty-five seconds?" I said, "No. I unpacked that in fifty years." That's the power of holding on to the truth and taking your identity deep. It changes you. It changes the way you live, the way you think, the way you feel, and the way you act, pray, and lead. I still occasionally visit the false platform of the people-pleasing lie, but I now live as a deeply loved person. And the deeper I take those roots, the greater my authority expands.

Let me tell you how that scene would have played out before I held on to the truth. Jen would have told me about the book, and I would have had an irrational reaction. We would have tiptoed around the house for a few days as if walking on eggshells. And eventually the tension would have lifted though we wouldn't have resolved the issue. We would have danced around our dysfunction. Eventually something else would have come up and triggered the same response, and we would have done the dance around dysfunction all over again—never really resolving the issue. But this time we had the conversation once, I steadied myself back on my proper foundation in Christ, and we never needed to have that conversation again. Once I lived on the false platform and occasionally visited the true platform of who I am in Christ, but now I live on the true platform and only occasionally visit the false one. And that has made all the difference in our relationship and in my spiritual authority.

Spiritual authority is rooted in identity. I knew these truths about who I was in Christ. I knew that God loved me; I preached this truth regularly. I believed it. But I wasn't always living from the place that I am a deeply loved, chosen child of God. My self-talk, my imaginary conversations, my defensiveness, and a host of other thoughts, feelings, and behaviors all betrayed the fact that knowing something isn't living it.

Too often we think, "I know this. I've got this. I'm loved by God. Yup." But if we aren't living as deeply loved children of God, then our identity is not rooted, and our authority is stunted. Our identity doesn't get rooted without intentionality. Passivity will not lead to authority. We must hold to the truth and take it deeper into our souls. We need the revelation of the Spirit to take us deep. The more we know we are deeply loved by God, the deeper we grow in our intimacy with Him.

But there is also this: spiritual authority is expanded in intimacy. That's what we'll look at in the next chapter.

FIVE:
EXPANDED IN INTIMACY

Wherever Jesus showed up in the New Testament, kingdom stuff happened. The blind would see, the deaf would hear, the mute would talk, the lame would walk, the demonized would be delivered. Hebrews tells us that Jesus hasn't changed: "Jesus Christ is the same yesterday and today and forever" (13:8). It's pretty simple, really: when Jesus shows up, amazing things happen. When I show up, however, nothing much happens. Jesus said, "Apart from me, you can do nothing" (John 15:5). I need to draw near to Jesus so my life can be marked by the presence of Jesus if I want to see the things of Jesus happen around me. The more I learn to attend to the presence of Jesus, carry the presence of Jesus, and walk in step with Jesus, the more likely kingdom happenings will characterize my journey.

After studying the life of Moses, I knew the one irrepressible need of my life was the presence of God. If you want to do the impossible, if you want to touch Heaven and change earth, if you want to move mountains, you must develop authority by drawing near to God. *Spiritual authority is rooted in identity and expanded in intimacy.* Of course, in many ways this was not a new discovery for me. From the earliest days of my ministry, I made a commitment to spend time with God. But I had more often sought His hands, not His face, and after reading the Moses account at the monastery, I made the shift. My heart started longing for intimacy with God; I longed for more of His presence. Authority flows out of intimacy. Seeking God's hands doesn't develop intimacy with God. If we are going to go deep with God, we must seek His face.

Our relationship with God is similar to our intimate human relationships. If I want to get closer to my wife, I can't always come seeking her hands; I must seek her for herself. If every time I talked to Jen I asked her to do things for me, our relationship would, naturally, be stunted.

> Seeking God's hands doesn't develop intimacy with God. If we are going to go deep with God, we must seek His face.

We wouldn't grow closer. But all too often this was what my relationship with God looked like: I came every day in prayer asking for what I needed. I was keenly aware of my need for God—His wisdom, His provision, His power, His anointing, His help in my life and the life of those I loved—so I spent time with Him daily. But I needed to shift my approach to pursuing Him for Himself. And I needed to intensify my pursuit of Him.

If we are going to draw near to God, we are going to have to spend time with Him—to be with Him, to get to know Him. There are many books out there about using spiritual disciplines—Bible reading and meditation, prayer, fasting, silence, solitude, worship, and the like—to connect with God. I don't need to rewrite what has been written. So I will start by assuming that you have some regular practice of spending time with God. If that is not true now, this is the place to begin. Set aside time with God on a regular basis. But if you are already doing that, let's talk about how to take it deeper.

Jesus is always our model for life and ministry. So let's look to Jesus as we begin this chapter on intimacy with God. No one ever had more demands upon His time, saw more clearly the needs of people, had more people seek Him out, or had more compassion for people than Jesus. But somehow Jesus managed to live an incredibly busy, in-demand life and yet stay deeply connected to the Father while staying rested, replenished, and fruitful, and all with massive spiritual authority. How did He do it?

I have spent much of the past year considering that. Here are a few key principles I've observed in the life of Jesus that can help us live like Him in authentic spiritual authority.

Living in Intimacy: Do the Father's Bidding

First, Jesus lived an intimate, rested, and fruitful life because He only did what the Father told Him to do, and only said what the Father told him to say. We looked at this earlier from the Gospel of John (John 5:19 and following; John 7:16).

Jesus never took on His own assignment. Human need did not drive Jesus to action. Jesus had compassion for human need, and He often ministered to people who came to Him with need. But Jesus responded to the Father's promptings, not to every presenting human need. This is important because human need is endless, and we are limited. If we respond to every need, we will burn out. We will end up saying yes to people's invitations to help and no to God's invitations to draw near. When Jesus came to a town, He knew people would come to Him with their sick and demonized. Often the Father's will was that He heal these sick and demonized people, and He joined the Father in His business. But He didn't go beyond the Father's will. When the Father told Him to move on to the next town, He did—even though, at times, He left sick and needy people behind. When the Father told Him to get away and rest and replenish, He did—even though some were left unhealed.

> So how do we decide what to do in a world of endless need? Jesus limited Himself to the Father's bidding. This is a wise approach because the Father knows your limitations better than you do.

We all have human limitations: we have limited time, energy, resources, gifts, and abilities, and we also have limited emotional and spiritual reserves. We cannot do everything. So how do we decide what to do in a world of endless need? Jesus limited Himself to the Father's bidding. This is a wise approach because the Father knows your limitations better than you do, and He knows where your time can be most wisely invested—better than you or others ever will. By the Father's directive, Jesus invested in the three, the Twelve, the seventy-two, the one hundred and twenty, and then, finally, the crowds. He did not make an equal investment in all of these groups; He invested far more in the three and the Twelve than He did the other groups. At times His unequal investment in some ignited jealousy in others, but Jesus did what the Father told Him to do. He wasn't seeking to be fair; He was seeking to be faithful. There were times Jesus left a village without meeting all the needs, as hard as that may have been for Him and as disappointing as it surely was for them.

Mark 1 tells the story of Jesus healing many people late into the night. The next day the whole town gathered at the door of Peter's mother-in-law's house to receive more from Jesus. There were still more needy, sick, hurting, and demonized people to attend to. Jesus, however, got up early the next day to be alone with His Father, and the disciples came looking for Him because the people had gathered again. But Jesus moved on from that place—leaving needy people behind—because that was what His Father was calling Him to do (Mark 1:29-39).

Everyone is worthy of love; not everyone is worthy of our investment. We can't invest in everyone; there is an unlimited amount of human need. Once God released me to write books, and travel more, I started becoming more visible and I had to pay close attention to my boundaries. I get requests from all over the world from people who have read *Soul Care* and are asking me to do their deliverance or help them in some way. Today, there are so many ways to contact a public figure—emails, FaceBook messages, Twitter, LinkedIn, Instagram, and more—and people need help. I can feel the desperation in their communication. I want to help, but I cannot respond to every communication or meet every need. I am extremely limited, and it is simply impossible. The Father's assignment for me is to equip people to do this ministry, not just to do Soul Care ministry or deliverance myself. If I do deliverance on individuals throughout my lifetime, thousands will be set free. If I equip leaders to do deliverance throughout my lifetime, hundreds of thousands will be set free. So I seek to do what the Father tells me to do. It doesn't always please people, and it often pains me, but it is for the greater good. Even though you aim for the good, it often feels bad when you are saying no, so you have to keep the larger picture in view: What is the Father asking you to do?

If we don't learn to say yes to the Father and no to people, we will end up spiritually anemic, emotionally depleted, and mostly ineffective. We will feel like Bilbo Baggins, who said in *The Fellowship of the Ring,* "I feel thin, sort of stretched, like butter scraped over too much bread."[6] We will end up ministering out of our humanity and not overflowing from and with God's presence. There are many times when, if we say yes to people, we will necessarily be saying no to the Father. And that is the wrong choice for our soul, for His kingdom, and ultimately for those people. We cannot live an intimate, rested, and fruitful life without consistently saying yes to the Father and no to people when their request is outside the Father's directive. For us to know the Father's directive we must cultivate a still center where we can hear His voice and follow His promptings.

> Every battle is not your battle. Every need is not your responsibility. Every human request is not the Father's desire for you to meet. Do what the Father calls you to do.

Every battle is not your battle. Every need is not your responsibility. Every human request is not the Father's desire for you to meet. Do what the Father calls you to do.

The hard part is limiting yourself to the Father's bidding. It can be hard for us to say no to people; it can be hard for us to discern what the Father wants us to do.

Jesus discovered that doing His Father's will was food to His soul. For Jesus, doing the Father's will was replenishing, life-giving; it sustained Him. The disciples went to get lunch one day, and Jesus stayed behind to talk to a woman at a well (John 4). When the disciples came back they were surprised to find Jesus talking to a Samaritan woman. After she left, they offered Jesus food. He responded, "I have food to eat that you know nothing about. My food is to do the will of him who sent me and finish his work" (John 4:32-34). When Jesus did the work of the Father, He worked in the strength of the Father. The Father gave Jesus what He needed to do His Father's bidding. God will give us the strength to do His bidding, not our bidding or other people's bidding. We must be convinced that limiting ourselves to do the Father's bidding is food to our soul.

The number one job of a spiritual leader is to find the mind of Christ and do it. The problem is our motives often mess up our intention to do the Father's will. When we have shame, like Moses, it often fuels our drivenness and, in an attempt to prove ourselves, we take on more than God intended. When we have unprocessed people-pleasing in our soul, we say yes to people and no to the Father and we run out of divine supply. When we do more than the Father's desire, we work in our own energy and end up depleted emotionally and spiritually. We often become resentful that people demand so much of us. In reality, though, it is not their fault; we don't set firm boundaries because of our own inner issues. When the issue of our value is still unsettled and we are motivated by people-pleasing, we take on assignments that are outside the Father's plan. This is why it is so vital to be rooted in our identity in Christ.

We have to deal with our mixed motives if we are going to live within our limits.

We have to walk in step with the Father so we know what the Father is calling us to say yes to. We have to be secure in the Father's love to say no to everyone but the Father. We have to get to the place where we can say no without feeling guilty. I don't answer many emails or messages that come to me. I simply cannot keep up with all of them, and I had to get to the place where I could ignore the volume of messages I received without feeling guilty. I had to content myself with doing the Father's bidding.

I have found it helpful to clearly define the assignment God has for me and the calling of my life. Doing this helps me decide the Father's will in the face of many needs and opportunities. I couldn't do that as easily when I was younger, but the older I got, the clearer my assignment became. When you are younger you often have to serve as a generalist to figure out your gifts and calling, develop character and intimacy, and earn your stripes. But there comes a time, when you get older, when you should narrow the scope of your assignment. You should more clearly define what you are gifted at, passionate about, and called to. There comes a time when you are going to have to say no more than you say yes to people if you are to stay true to the Father's calling. The more fruit you bear, the more opportunities you will have, and the more difficult it becomes to sort out those opportunities. Defining a framework of the Father's call on your life makes sorting out those opportunities easier.

Here is my framework; I give it to you as an example to think through. (It is descriptive, but it is not prescriptive for anyone else's life.) God has called me to fight for renewal. I am to write, speak, and mentor leaders to help fight for revival.

I generally take assignments where I am called to speak on renewal subjects to pastors or large churches so I can multiply centers of influence, because that is part of the assignment God has given me. I am called to train and equip leaders in soul and Spirit on things that can help release renewal. Knowing that is what the Lord has called me to helps me make better and quicker decisions. I don't have to labor over every opportunity to serve. I say no to everything that doesn't fit God's assignment for my life. If someone calls me to do a marriage seminar, the answer is no. It isn't that I don't have things to teach on that subject; I do. I've learned a lot about marriage, but it doesn't fit the calling of my life. I've had people say to me, "You should write a book on parenting" or "do a book on marriage" or some other subject—but again, that isn't my calling. There are plenty of other people who are doing those things and doing them well. My calling, in all I do, is to fight for revival. Knowing your specific assignment from the Lord allows you to make quicker decisions. You have a grid to think through and you can eliminate a bunch of opportunities that are great opportunities, just not God's assignment for you.

When I was 24, I sought the Lord. He laid out His plan for my life: "You will plant a church. You will teach in seminary. You will write books and train leaders internationally. Everything you do will be to fight for renewal." I told the Lord, "I will do whatever you want me to do, but I will never open my own doors. You open the doors when you're ready, and I'll walk through them." I didn't want to pry open doors before their time because of my pride or ambition, so I committed to wait on God. And He was faithful; He opened the doors in His timing. That has been my life: one by one the doors opened and now I am literally living the dream; I am living the life the Lord called me to. I am having more fun and bearing more fruit in ministry than ever before. I am having the time of my life doing what God called me to.

Doing the Lord's will is food for the soul. If we can limit ourselves to God's assignment we will have God's strength to do it. Now every opportunity that comes in that fits my assignment to fight for renewal, I always do two things: I pray about, and then I try to discern if it is the mind of Christ. Jen has veto power to vote down any assignment I want to take but shouldn't. We don't get every decision right, but we get the vast majority right, and the fruit and joy in ministry is evident.

> Doing the Lord's will is food for the soul. If we can limit ourselves to God's assignment we will have God's strength to do it.

Are you committed to doing the Father's will? Are you praying through opportunities that come your way to discern the mind of Christ? Do you have a "calling grid" that allows you to think through decisions quickly? Find what God wants for you and do it.

Living in Intimacy: Lonely Places and Retreat Spaces

The second observation about Jesus' life of rest and fruitfulness is that He often withdrew to lonely places to be with His Father. We must understand the importance of retreat. Jesus retreated and taught His disciples to follow His example. In Mark 6:30, 31, after the disciples come back from a ministry assignment, Jesus gathers them together to hear their report. While doing that, He called them to retreat: "The apostles gathered around Jesus and told him all that they had done and taught. He said to them, 'Come away to a deserted place all by yourselves and rest a while.' For many were coming and going, and they had no leisure even to eat" (NRSV).

Jesus sent His disciples out on mission to cast out demons, heal the sick, and preach the kingdom. They came back and reported to Jesus all that happened. I wish I could have been at that coaching session! Then Jesus calls them to get away with Him and rest. I love Mark's description (6:32): "For many were coming and going, and they had no leisure even to eat." Now that's busy! He couldn't even get a bite to eat because He was in such demand. Sometimes I hear people say that Jesus lived a balanced life and Jesus wasn't busy, but that's not true. Jesus was busy, but rested, because He did what the Father told Him to do and He retreated for refueling. Retreats are refueling centers for the soul.

I was doing a Soul Care Conference in Winnipeg in the spring of 2019; there were about 350 people attending. On Saturday we did deliverance. There was a huge line of people waiting for deliverance. I had trained and equipped people in deliverance before coming, but they were fairly new at it, and when you are learning it is slow going. We were doing deliverances on the crowd from early afternoon until evening; we had a 7 p.m. service coming and there was not going to be a break. Finally, I asked someone, "Is there any food in the house?" Someone had ordered a pizza, so I literally ate pizza while I continued doing deliverance. I did deliverance right up until the evening service started.

It was later in the week that I read the passage above, from Mark. Jesus got that kind of ministry busyness. The people were desperate and constantly pressing Him for miraculous intervention. There was no leisure, even to eat, so he took retreats to get away from the crowds and be alone with His

Father and friends. The more you carry the presence of God, the more in demand you will be, the busier you are, the more you will need to get away from the crowds to be alone with the Father. Retreating was an essential part of Jesus' replenishing strategy.

As I've been studying the life of Jesus through Mark this year, I've noticed how often Jesus got away from the crowds. Look with me:

- Mark 1:35: "In the morning, while it was still very dark, he got up and went out to a deserted place, and there he prayed."

- Mark 3:7: "Jesus departed with his disciples to the sea . . . " This was one of Jesus' favorite escape routes. He often got in a boat to retreat because no one could follow Him there and He could rest and replenish.

- Mark 3:13, 14: "He went up to the mountain and called to him those whom he wanted, and they came to him. And he appointed twelve, whom he also named apostles, to be with him, and he sent them out to proclaim the message." Jesus also used mountains a great deal to get away. Luke 6:12 tells us He spent the night on a mountain praying to God. Another of Jesus' favorite retreating strategies was to pray in the hours of darkness when everyone else was asleep. Retreats are acts of sacrifice; they are a costly but necessary practice for those who want to carry His presence. And notice that He also calls the disciples to be with Him as He was with the Father. Abiding through retreat space is a major theme in Jesus' life.

- Mark 6:45, 46: "Immediately he made his disciples get into the boat and go ahead to the other side, to Bethsaida, while he dismissed the crowd. After saying farewell to them, he went up on the mountain to pray."

- Mark 7:24: "From there he set out and went away to the region of Tyre. He entered a house and did not want anyone to know he was there. Yet he could not escape notice." Notice that Jesus didn't want anyone to notice He was in the house. Often when Jesus tried to get away, the crowds found him and pressed Him for help. It wasn't easy to retreat. That is why He used boats, mountains, darkness, and lonely places.

- Mark 7:33: "He took him [a deaf man] aside in private, away from the crowd . . . "

- Mark 9:2: "Six days later, Jesus took with him Peter and James and John, and led them up by a high mountain apart, by themselves."

- Mark 9:30: "They went on from there and passed through Galilee. He did not want anyone to know it."

Jesus practiced retreat because He could do nothing apart from the Father—he said this clearly and in His own words. Luke 5:16: "Jesus often withdrew to lonely places and he prayed." This was His regular practice to get retreat space away from the crowds. When you read the Gospels, though, you see that it was hard for Jesus to get away. Just as Jesus could do nothing apart from the Father, we can do nothing apart from Jesus (John 15), so we too must make a habit of retreating. We must get alone with God enough to abide in the Vine, or we will wither and bear little fruit.

There are some places I cannot get to in my relationship with God in my daily time with God. There are some depths I cannot experience without block times alone with the Father.

This is one of the benefits of retreating. But retreating also allows us to replenish the drain of ministry and life's demands. As we meet with people, and pour out, our spiritual energy slowly drains. Retreats allow us to replenish the tank. Jesus needed it; how much more the rest of us?

Jesus also got away from the crowds because they were draining. I don't think I have ever appreciated the humanity of Jesus like I do after meditating my way through Mark's gospel in the past year. Jesus got away from the crowds because He was drained; He hit His limits and needed to retreat. That's the reality of ministry. Ministry is draining. When you are meeting people's needs, ministering to people's pain, and praying for people's requests, you feel the drain physically, spiritually, and emotionally.

> Retreats allow us to replenish the tank. Jesus needed it; how much more the rest of us?

When I do Soul Care Conferences, I am often ministering twelve hours a day for three days, and it is draining. It isn't just physically tiring; I am expending emotional and spiritual resources, too, as I listen to people's painful stories, minister to people's souls, and cast out demons. Sometimes on the last day I am doing deliverance, and there are still people left in line, but I can't keep doing it. I hit the wall—the interior wall of my human limits—and I'm done. I've spent everything there is to spend and the tank is empty. I look at people and say, "I'm sorry, but I'm done." I have set people up and trained them before I came, so they will get ministry in the days to come. But I can't do any more because I am a real person with real limitations. We need to honor our limits, and that means we need to withdraw from the crowds and replenish. We need to retreat like Jesus did.

Sabbath Rest

Sabbath rest is a form of retreat. I want to talk about the concept of the Sabbath, but I am not going to present it the way the Sabbath is typically presented. You may disagree with my thinking about this matter, but be gracious and hear my heart on the subject. When I read the gospels, I don't see clear evidence that Jesus practices the Sabbath in a traditional way. That is, I don't think He took every Saturday or Sunday off. There are plenty of stories where the Pharisees are upset with Jesus because He is doing work on the Sabbath—healing the sick, for example—and they complain to Jesus that He is violating the Sabbath. It is one of the things that annoys the Pharisees the most: Jesus seems to disregard their understanding of the Sabbath.

John 5 records one of those examples, and when the Pharisees complain that Jesus is working on the Sabbath, He responds, "My Father is always at his work to this very day, and I too am working" (John 5:17). Now don't get me wrong: it is clear that Jesus practiced retreat—He got away to rest and replenish, to restore—and this is Sabbath rest. But that retreat didn't necessarily look like a weekly day off. I know there are lots of people who argue for a weekly Sabbath day, and I think that is ideal, but I can't say that I see that as I study the life of Jesus in the gospels. I am not arguing for an irresponsible drivenness that leads to breakdown. I definitely see that Jesus practices Sabbath in the form of regular retreat and healthy rhythms. But as I have studied the gospels, I am not convinced that the retreat looks like a weekly Sabbath day without work like many proponents of Sabbath rest write about.

As a result, I have come to think of the principle of Sabbath a little differently, but, I would argue, not wrongly. When I was a pastor, I fit my schedule into a weekly rhythm with a weekly day off, and I took a Sabbath day on Saturday. And that worked well for many years. But even then I began to think about Sabbath rest in terms of a longer calendar—not just a weekly rhythm, but a yearly rhythm. In the Old Testament there was a law that allowed the land to rest every seventh year. It was a year of Sabbath for the land. So they too had a broader understanding of Sabbath rest, one beyond merely a weekly rhythm. I started thinking about Sabbath rest on a year-long calendar; I needed enough retreat space in my schedule over the course of a year to stay rested and replenished. I needed enough space so that my inputs could balance my outputs and I wasn't being depleted.

The reality is that sometimes the drain is not taking place on a weekly basis, but the drain on our souls is like a slow leak in a tire over time. It isn't a blowout, but one day, if you don't pay attention to the slow leak, you will have a flat tire. I had to make sure there was sufficient time alone with the Lord in my calendar so the flow of the Spirit into my life was greater than the flow of the Spirit out of my life. This became increasingly important as the ministry opportunities and demands were expanding in my life.

So I began thinking of Sabbath in a larger way, one beyond merely a weekly rhythm of a day of rest. Sabbath doesn't always look like a weekly day off for me; that isn't always possible with my lifestyle. But I do practice regular days off, retreat days, and I strive for a healthy rhythm. I think the principle of the Sabbath is a principle of rest, and I believe it is vital to a replenished, spiritually full, sustainable lifestyle. However, thinking of Sabbath over a yearly rhythm is a much better way for me personally to consider it given the call of God on my life. Let me describe my rhythm of rest. But again, let me say: this is not prescriptive for anyone else's lifestyle; I am merely trying to describe what I am doing as I try to honor my limits and the principle of Sabbath rest I find in Scripture and modeled in Jesus' life.

I try to get a day off each week, but with traveling around the world, that doesn't always work. Sometimes my "day off" is a travel day. And, I can assure you, that is not a day of rest even though I am not working. I often use the time in the plane to be alone with God and to replenish my emotional tank, but it sure doesn't feel like a retreat day or a day of rest, especially as we now cross time zones so easily. I try to get a few days off each month where I am not working and I'm not en route to some new location.

I am also trying to set aside at least one day each month where I get alone with God to spiritually retreat, replenish, and restore. That is a day off, not just for recreation or fun, but a day alone with God. It is a day to linger in His presence, to seek His face. It is a long, slow day lingering with God, and I need these block times alone with God to go deep with Him. I can't get where I want to go in intimacy with God on a maintenance schedule of just an hour or two a day alone with God.

I also take about six weeks off each summer to retreat. As I write this chapter, I am on my summer break. My theme for the summer is rest, ride, and write. I take more days off just to have fun, be with family, enjoy the nice weather, visit friends, go to fun places, and rest. This kind of rest is emotionally replenishing; it fills my soul. It allows me to take in the goodness of God and feel His joy and pleasure. I also spend a block of time alone with God to start each day during these six weeks; I have a long, slow time lingering with God in the morning. After my block of time with the Lord in the morning, I go for a ride on my bike. This is replenishing to me physically. I love being outdoors and I love riding my bike to exercise. I feel better when I am in shape. I have more energy; it helps me manage stress, and I can eat more! Then I take the afternoons to write. Writing is good for my soul; I love to write. It is a different work than speaking or ministering to people. It is refreshing to me. I look forward to it, and I find it joyfully replenishing.

By the time my summer sabbatical is over I will feel refreshed, renewed, and replenished physically, emotionally, and spiritually. Actually, I already do, and I'm only two weeks into my break as I write this. I also fast breakfast and lunch on my summer writing days. People often look at my schedule in, say, March or September and say, "You can't live like that. That's not sustainable." And that is true—but they are not looking at the larger picture of sabbath rest that takes place over the course of a year. The yearlong view is replenishing and sustainable.

I know a lot of people will read this and say, "That's great for you, but I can't do that. I have to work; I can't take that much time off." Everybody has to live the life God has assigned them. I didn't and couldn't always live like this either. But I didn't use to travel this much, and God made it very clear to me that He was calling me to travel—this was part of my assignment, and travel takes a lot out of me. And with the amount of travel I do, there has to be some time to catch up and restore—similar to the sabbath rest for the land. So I take the summer of sabbath rest that allows me to be fruitful and rested over the course of the year.

I travel about one-third of the time because that is what I sense the Lord is calling me to, and it works for Jen and me. I don't get a weekly day off every week, but I get regular time off, monthly retreat days, and a summer break that makes up for a lot of time away. This is enough to carry me. At this point, I feel free and full. I am having more fun and seeing more fruit in ministry than ever before, and that's a good sign that my rhythm is working. Jen and I are more happily married than we have ever been, and that's a good sign that it's working for Jen too.

Here is the larger point: You have to monitor your time with God. No one else will ever monitor that for you, or your level of soul health, or your spiritual well-being. Only you. You must figure out what works for you within the call of God on your life. We shouldn't emulate someone else's rhythm, nor should we condemn them. The big question is this: Have you been intentional in developing a spiritual rhythm so you can abide in Christ? Does your current rhythm work for you? Are you feeling free and full? Are you living deeply connected with God while you are fulfilling His assignments for your life? Do you have enough inputs to match the outputs? My rhythm works for me, for my calling, for my lifestyle, and for my family. But it wouldn't work for everybody, and it isn't anybody else's calling.

> Here is the larger point: You have to monitor your time with God. No one else will ever monitor that for you, or your level of soul health, or your spiritual well-being.

We all need enough retreat space and times with God to allow us to stay vitally connected to Jesus, because apart from Him we can do nothing. I cannot tell you how many times I am at a conference and I am spent spiritually and emotionally, and someone will come up to me and say, "I know you're tired, but . . . " Translation: "I know you're tired, but it doesn't matter. I am desperately in need and you can help me." I have to monitor my limits and you must monitor yours. Not everyone has the same capacity, not everyone has the same schedule, not everyone has the same calling. But everyone does have limits, and everyone needs to stay connected to the Vine. You have to figure out what it takes to make that happen in your life.

I like to think of my rhythm like this: What do I need on a daily, weekly, monthly, and yearly basis to stay vitally connected to Jesus? Jesus said the Holy Spirit is like a river within us (John 7:37). I want to consistently live in the River of God. Where the River of God flows, everything lives (Ezekiel 47:9). I have to stay in the River of God's presence to access the abundant life of Jesus. I have to stay in the River of God if I am going to carry the presence of God to people around me. If what you are doing is keeping you consistently in the River, then keep it up! If you feel an ever-deepening connection with God, you are sensing His love, hearing His voice, feeling His peace, experiencing His favor, and seeing the fruit of the Spirit in your life, then stick with your rhythm. If you are carrying a sense of His presence and increasing in your capacity to touch Heaven and change earth, then keep going! But if you are finding yourself depleted spiritually and emotionally spent, and sensing an increasing distance from God and others, then you need to make adjustments to your rhythm.

Changing Rhythm

When I have to make an adjustment to my rhythm, I go to the Lord and ask for wisdom. What should I do differently? How should I tweak my rhythm so I can be intimate, rested, and fruitful? Years back I went through a depleting season in ministry. I went to the monastery at the end of the year for an annual retreat. As I spent time with the Lord there, I sensed the refreshing of the Lord, I was replenished spiritually and emotionally, and I felt the Lord telling me to start going on a spiritual retreat every two months. I did what the Lord told me to do and it changed my life. I got to a depth with God that I never could have reached without regular retreats.

It isn't easy to adjust your rhythm, but as your life changes it is often needed to adjust your rhythm to ensure you stay in the River. This new season of travel in my life was clearly confirmed by God—multiple times. The Lord had given me a clear call to this when I was 24, as I shared earlier. Then one Christmas while I was spending time alone with the Lord, I sensed Him say to me, "It is time to travel." I knew that day had been coming and, at that point, the Lord was telling me it was here. I said, "If that's you, confirm it. I'll do whatever you ask." Three people came to me in the next two weeks and said they had visions or dreams of me traveling, and these were not people given to dreams and visions! It was clearly confirmed from God, and then the invitations started coming. I didn't seek them out, they just came.

But the new season of travel meant I had to give up my bi-monthly monastery retreats. I couldn't continue going to the monastery every two months while I was away a third of the time on the road; it would have been too hard on my family and me. So I had to come up with a new rhythm. The new plan, as I mentioned, is to have one day each month where I sit on my porch overlooking the lake by my house and spend a day alone with God, and I couple this with the summer sabbatical where I spend half a day each day alone with God.

All new rhythms must be evaluated, and they can't be evaluated without the passing of time. I haven't done this new rhythm long enough to tell if it will work over the long haul. Sometimes you have a slow leak in your spiritual well-being. Like a tire on a car, sometimes we start to slowly lose air in our spiritual tire, but we don't notice it. We need a change in rhythm, but we don't realize it because there hasn't been a drastic shift in spiritual air pressure. So far, so good—I feel free, full, fruitful, and I'm having fun doing it all. I'm actually having the time of my life in ministry. But I am also aware that I need to monitor this new rhythm over the next year or so to see if it works long term. If I sense the tire starting to get a little flat, I'll have to make another adjustment. It won't be the first adjustment I've made to my spiritual rhythm, and it won't be the last.

How about you? Are you getting enough spiritual air in the tire of your soul? Are you living in the River of God? Are you free, full, and fruitful, and are you having fun while you're doing it? If so, you're probably in a good space. If not, what adjustment in your rhythm could help you gain spiritual air in your tire? Ask the Lord. Wait on Him. Take a day to pray and fast and seek Him for direction. What could you do differently on a daily, weekly, monthly, and/or yearly basis to help your spir-

> Are you living in the River of God? Are you free, full, and fruitful, and are you having fun while you're doing it?

itual connectivity and take you to a deeper place with God? When you develop a new rhythm, be sure to build in a few spots along the way where you can stop and evaluate if the new rhythm is working.

You will also discover that there are certain difficult seasons in your life that tax your reserves. You cannot continue your regular rhythm during those seasons because you are more drained by the grief or hardship you are facing, so you need to adjust your rhythm in seasons like that in order to stay in the River of God.

But there is a danger to a spiritual rhythm, and this is it: When your routine becomes a rut, you become religious. Often, we can develop a spiritual rhythm, get comfortable with it, and actually start stagnating, because of our comfort, without realizing it. If we are going to develop our authority, we must expand our intimacy. Stagnation will not get us there; stagnation will not move those mountains before us.

Breaking Spiritual Ruts

A couple of things help with stagnation. First, I have to change my spiritual activities. For example, I can't keep worshiping to the same old song. I need to sing a new song. When I can sing a song and think about something else while I'm singing it, it's time for new music. It has to ignite passion in my heart; it has to connect me to the heart of the Father.

I was challenged when I was young to read through the Bible in a year, so I started reading three to four chapters a day. But if that is all I do, it becomes a rut for me. Sometimes I need to read Scripture, sometimes I need to pray the Scriptures, sometimes I need to study the Scriptures, sometimes I need to meditate on a small section at a time. If I change it up, I have a much better chance of keeping it fresh and staying out of the rut.

I've also found that often in my relationship with God, to get to a new level of intimacy, I have to sacrifice. Sometimes I stagnate because I am stuck, and often the best way out of my plateau is sacrifice. Jesus began His ministry with a forty-day fast in the wilderness. Sacrifice. There have been times I felt stuck in my level of intimacy and I knew that, to get to the next level, I needed to go on a longer fast. This is one of the reasons I fast and pray over my summer sabbatical break. I only fast and pray when I am writing, Monday to Friday, and only breakfast and lunch, but it is part of my regular rhythm of fasting over the course of a year that's designed to help me go deeper with God (and also to help with fresh inspiration in the writing process). If Jesus, the perfect, sinless Son of God needed to fast, how much more you and I? Jesus said to His disciples, in the Sermon on the Mount, "When you fast . . . " (Matthew 6:16). Not if.

In the first Great Awakening, Wesley and his friends fasted two days a week; it was just part of their regular rhythm of seeking God. I think it is beneficial to have a regular rhythm of fasting. It may involve a weekly fast of twenty-four hours (going without food from dinner one night until dinner the next), and it may involve a period of fasting at some point during the year. You may fast for three days, or a week or longer, once or twice per year. I like my summer rhythm of fasting, but I may also sense the Lord calling me to fast for a week during the year at some point to get to a new breakthrough in intimacy with Him, or for some other reason. Is fasting part of your yearly rhythm? If not, why not build it into that rhythm? The Lord said, "When you fast . . . " Take Him up on His call and fast for new intimacy depths with Him.

Just as there are some spiritual places with God I could not have gotten to without retreating, there are places I could not have reached without fasting. Fasting is vital for depth; fasting is essential for breakthrough. Fasting is one form of sacrifice that helps us expand intimacy and develop authority. But it isn't the only path forward.

After God led me to study Moses and revealed I needed to increase my pursuit of intimacy, I went away to the monastery on one of my regularly scheduled bimonthly retreats. I had a couple of friends with me. I sensed the Lord leading me to stay up all night and pray. I prayed with my friends before bedtime, and Tommy asked what I was going to do after we finished praying. I told him I was going to stay up all night and pray. Tommy was our church's youth pastor—a typical youth guy—so he was up for an all-nighter. He said, "Can I join you?" I said, "Sure. You don't have to. I feel called by God to stay up all night." But he wanted to. He and I started meeting once a week to stay up into the wee hours of the night to pursue God. Others found out and joined us. At one point we had about fifty people gathering on a Friday night to pursue God into the wee hours of the night. Those periods of sacrificing sleep were essential for a new level in my intimacy with God. God honors sacrifice.

David talked about night watches. Psalm 63:6: "On my bed I remember you; I think of you through the watches of the night." This isn't the only time that idea occurs in the Psalms. The monasteries picked up on this Scriptural theme, and some monks and others staying in monasteries will get up in the night every night to pray. They have a night watch. It's not uncommon to have the Lord wake me up in the middle of the night when I'm traveling. These wake-up calls from the Lord have been critically important to my expanding intimacy and developing authority.

Many years ago, I was teaching a class at Alliance Theological Seminary in New York, and the Lord woke me up at 2 a.m. I got out of bed in response to his wake-up call, and I heard the Spirit speak to my heart: "This class is full of demons." I have a funny relationship with God; I make humorous comments to Him sometimes when I pray. He thinks I'm funny, and so do I. So I said to Him, "You woke me up at 2 a.m. to tell me that? That could have waited until 6 a.m.!" He retorted, "There are some things I only say to my 2 a.m. friends!" Touché. He thinks He is funny too—and so do I.

Little did I know that this 2 a.m. wake-up call would change my life forever. I asked the Lord, "What do you want me to do?" He said, "I want you to do a group test." I had been doing deliverances for many years at that point, but until then I had been doing them all one at a time as pastoral appointments. But that middle-of-the-night conversation launched me into doing tests on groups of people and also doing multiple deliverances at a time—at first dozens of people in the group, and now sometimes hundreds at a time.

From responding to that 2 a.m. wake-up call and obeying the prompting of the Spirit, my spiritual authority began to dramatically increase. If you do dozens of deliverances, you will develop authority. If you do hundreds of deliverances, you will grow more. But when you start doing thousands of deliverances across many cultures, your spiritual authority will grow exponentially. I started equipping people to do deliverance, and my authority was rapidly expanding. That prompting changed my life. I don't believe people should start doing group tests until the Lord brings them to that level—every battle is not your battle, every need is not your responsibility,

> Every battle is not your battle, every need is not your responsibility, every opportunity is not your assignment. Do what the Father calls you to do.

every opportunity is not your assignment. Do what the Father calls you to do. The Father called me to that step, and it changed me forever and has resulted in thousands of people getting free.

When I first started doing deliverances, I got stuck a lot. I would get into a situation I had never faced, and I didn't know what to do. I would fast and pray and wait on God for revelation. He would hand me a new key to the kingdom, a new revelation to unlock human bondage, and it would expand my authority.

This is the power of sacrifice. When we sacrifice to get up in the night to pray, or we sacrifice by prayer and fasting for intimacy or revelation, or we block out times away with God on retreat, we can develop our intimacy and expand our authority. Nothing has helped my intimacy with God expand more than sacrificial acts, particularly retreats. Doing a monastery retreat every two months for more than a decade has deepened me with God like nothing else I've done. If you are thinking about getting away, even for half a day, put it on the calendar. We are all well-intentioned but busy people, and if we don't put it on our calendar, it won't happen. Other things will creep in and rob you of that well-intentioned re-

> When you pursue Him, you find Him in new depths. It doesn't all happen at once, but if you persist, you will find Him.

treat space. If I don't lock in the summer break, it will never happen—I have enough requests to fill my calendar all year long. But even Jesus needed to retreat to live a replenished and fruitful life. How much more do we?

What sacrifice is the Father calling you to make to get to your next level with God? Often these sacrifices fuel my desire for God. Your intimacy can never rise above your level of desire for God. When you fuel your desire, you pursue Him. When you pursue Him, you find Him in new depths. It doesn't all happen at once, but if you persist, you will find Him.

Living in Intimacy: Drawing from God's Strength

Third, Jesus lived an intimate, rested, and fruitful life because He drew from His Father's strength. Divine union with His Father was His supernatural source of strength. It gave Him capacity to exceed His human limits. Jesus' food was to do His Father's will; it fed His soul. He only did what the Father told Him to do; He only said what the Father told Him to say. He could do nothing apart from the Father, and His union with the Father was the source of His strength and rest.

Jesus invites us into that same sort of relationship with Him. Jesus said, "I and the Father are one" (John 10:30). He prayed, "My prayer is not for them [the Twelve] alone. I pray also for those who will believe in me through their message, that all of them may be one, Father, just as you are in me and I am in you. May they also be in us so that the world may believe that you have sent me" (John 17:20, 21). Jesus was in the Father; the Father was in Jesus. This was their divine union. And Jesus invites us into that union. That we would be united with them.

Just as Jesus could do nothing apart from His Father, so He told us we could do nothing apart from Him. We have to learn to live in this same divine union and draw from His strength. John 15:4, 5: "Abide in me as I abide in you. Just as the branch cannot bear fruit by itself unless it abides in the vine, neither can you unless you abide in me. I am the vine; you are the branches. Those who abide in me and I in them bear much fruit; apart from me you can do nothing." Notice that the command in the passage is to abide, not to bear fruit. Fruit-bearing is a by-product. If we abide, we will bear fruit. Yet, too often our focus is on bearing fruit, not on abiding. We work really hard in an attempt to bear fruit, but Jesus calls us to abide. Abiding needs to be our number one priority; abiding needs to be the overarching theme of our lives if we want to be kingdom fruit-bearers. If we focus on our plans, our ideas, our strategies, and do it with our gifts, abilities, and competencies, we will accomplish what we can accomplish. But if we want to see what God can accomplish, we must abide. This is the only way to expand our authority. When we abide, we carry His presence. We carry His presence into our problems. We carry His presence into our appointments. And when Jesus shows up, kingdom stuff happens. Supernatural fruit cannot be borne with human effort. Supernatural fruit can only be borne with abiding and divine enablement. When our connection to the Vine causes His presence to saturate our lives, kingdom fruit is much more likely to happen.

If we are going to go deeper with God, we must spend time with Him. We can't grow closer to a friend without being with them, and it is not different with God. He too is a person. We practice spiritual disciplines that help us connect with God and assist us in abiding. This is why we worship, read our Bibles, pray Scripture, meditate on Scripture, fast, seek His face, spend time in solitude and silence, journal, and more. These practices are not to be an end in themselves; they help us practice His presence—and to abide in Christ.

We must engage in these spiritual practices with the right attitude or they can actually lead us farther from God. The purpose of reading the Bible is not to know the Bible; the purpose of reading the Bible is to have a fresh encounter with the living God. The purpose of praying is not to say what is on our mind; the purpose of praying is to abide in Christ. The Pharisees did all the right religious practices, and they killed Jesus. If we abide, we can learn how to draw from His reserves when the time comes. We can't draw from the Vine if we're not connected.

> The purpose of reading the Bible is not to know the Bible; the purpose of reading the Bible is to have a fresh encounter with the living God.

In the spring of 2019, I was out doing ministry for at least part of ten weekends in a row on top of my regular seminary teaching schedule two days per week. I was in the seventh straight weekend out and I could sense I had hit a wall. When I hit a wall emotionally and/or spiritually I have come to the end of my human limits. I usually feel some angst in my soul; it is like my insides start to vibrate. I came home from the weekend and figured I had enough time to replenish before I went away for the next weekend. I spent time alone with the Lord, but the wall didn't come down. I said to Jen, just before I left for my eighth weekend, "I'm in trouble. I have three more weekends to go in this ministry stretch, all Soul Care weekends, which are particularly draining on me, and I've hit a wall. And I didn't break through it this week while I was alone with God."

I told the host when I got there that I had hit a wall and needed a room to escape to where I could sit alone with God during breaks. I had been meditating on Psalm 116 periodically over the course of the previous nine or ten months. The Psalmist writes in verse 7, "Return, O my soul, to your rest; for the Lord has dealt bountifully with you" (NRSV). I remember one day meditating on it, and these words escaped my lips: "I draw from your strength." I knew it was a Holy Spirit-inspired phrase. As I meditated on the passage it occurred to me that we only lose our rest when we lose sight of the Lord's bounty in our life. When we lose sight of the Lord's bountiful provision, we lose our rest and become fearful of our finances. When we lose sight of the Lord's bountiful peace, we lose our rest and become overwhelmed by our circumstances. When we lose sight of the Lord's bountiful love, we become consumed with the opinions of others.

As I came to that eighth weekend away the Holy Spirit reminded me of this verse I had been meditating on, and I knew there was a reserve in Christ I had not yet tapped. So I had asked the pastor for that retreat prayer room during breaks. Every fifteen-minute break I sat alone with the Lord in that prayer room and meditated on Psalm 116:7. I sat in silence and drew from his strength. I actually gained ground as the weekend went on. While I was ministering, I broke through the wall and ended up with more energy, more peace, and no angst by the time the weekend ended. And I sailed through the next two weekends in the same way.

My tribe is the Christian and Missionary Alliance. A.B. Simpson, our founder, often wrote about "the Christ life." He talked about this divine enablement that is available to us all.

I experienced it like never before in the spring of 2019. Here's an analogy: for years I drove a motorcycle that had a 3.5-gallon tank. When that tank was empty, however, I wasn't done for; the bike had a reserve tank. I would be riding and all of a sudden the engine would sputter because it was running out of gas, and I would reach down and flip a switch and the engine would access the reserve tank. And I would get another twenty or thirty miles, which would get me to a gas station.

Jesus learned to draw from His Father's strength. There is enough strength in divine union to do all the assignments the Father has for us. But we must learn how to draw from His strength as we abide in Him. If we limit ourselves to what the Father asks us to do, as Jesus did, we can claim the promise for divine enablement for that assignment. Even when we hit our human limits, there is a reserve tank for the divine enablement.

Now, we can't abuse this. It has to be the Father's assignment, and it doesn't make up for the need to retreat and engage in spiritual disciplines that allow us to abide. We must abide; the divine enablement comes out of abiding, but part of abiding is drawing from His strength, when we discover we are doing the Father's will but we hit our capacity. There is more. But there has to be a baseline of abiding before we can draw from His strength. When we hit empty on the Father's tasks, however, it is encouraging to know there is a reserve tank in the heavenlies for those who abide.

Three Attitudes for Abiding

Remember: When your routine becomes a rut, you become religious. So we must keep our spiritual activities fresh so they refresh us in God's presence. Doing spiritual disciplines and

> Remember: When your routine becomes a rut, you become religious.

participating in spiritual activities is not the same as abiding. The key to keeping these spiritual actions fresh and replenishing so often comes down to our attitude. Let me explain three key attitudes we must have as we spend time with God.

First: Being, Not Doing

First, as we spend time alone with God, we must make it about being, not about doing. Too often we can become dutiful Christians who have a "to-do list." In order to be good and faithful Christians we need to read our Bibles, pray, go to church, tithe, serve, and other essential things. But you and I have both faithfully picked up our Bible to read it, read two chapters, and all of a sudden realized we had no idea what we were reading because our mind was not paying attention to the text. We are doing our duty, but we are not engaging with God. We've all done it. This isn't helping us grow closer to God; this is just being religious. If we are going to read our Bible with intimacy, we can't just read the chapters because it is something we are supposed to do as good Christians. Reading the Bible without encountering God in the text is not going to expand our intimacy with the Father.

Sometimes I watch people at restaurants, and I will see a couple out on a date. They are spending time together, they are out together, but they aren't connecting. They are both on their phones, or they sit in silence, and you can feel the tension and distance between them as you watch. They are going through the motions, but they aren't drawing near. The same thing can happen to me and you in our relationship with God.

We have to make it about being, not about doing. We have come to meet with God, to *be with* Him. We have to make sure our heart is prepared; our attitude is focused on being with Him.

As we pick up our Bible, we have to remind ourselves that we are one Holy Spirit breath away from a fresh encounter with the Living God, and we focus on meeting Him and wait for Him to breathe on the passage. We read the text with attentiveness to His presence in the passage. We are looking for the moment when the Spirit breathes on the passage and stirs something in our hearts; we are looking for the opportunity to meet God in Scripture. Where is He speaking to me? What is it that grabs my attention? Where do I sense the Spirit stirring my heart? How is God revealing Himself to me in the text? Is there a phrase, a word, that leaps off the page? The morning I wrote this, for example, I was meditating on Mark 10:46-52, and I was struck by Bartimaeus's desperation that produced such faith within him. Desperation is often the platform to break through because it makes us throw ourselves with abandon on God; we have nowhere else to turn. People tried to shut Bartimaeus up, but he would have none of it. He was too desperate. "Jesus, Son of David, have mercy on me!" That's the cry of the desperate. And, so often, it is also the birthplace of deep faith.

I have a situation that is pretty desperate in my life right now, a mountain I need God to move, and in that encounter with the text I sensed the Spirit stirring me to the faith of Bartimaeus. I met the Jesus that Bartimaeus met that day.

Second: Attending to His Presence

Second, our attitude as we pursue God for intimacy must be about attending to His presence. Brother Lawrence talked about practicing the presence of God. He was able to become aware of God in the sanctuary in worship and in the kitchen peeling potatoes. Frank Laubach picked up on this theme and wrote about it as well. I am inspired by the life and writings of these two men, but I have to confess it is much more difficult for me to live in the continuous awareness of God's presence. For me, it is much easier in the sanctuary or in my prayer closet to practice the presence of God than it is as I go through daily routines. But sometimes a change in words can lead to a change in attitude. So I started using the phrase "attend to His presence."

I want to attend to His presence in worship. That means I don't always sing, because the purpose of worship isn't really to sing songs, it is to bring my full attention to God and love Him as He deserves. Sometimes singing can actually distract me from His presence. Sometimes it is better for me just to focus on His presence, and as I attend to His presence it feeds my soul and I love Him afresh. I try to attend to His presence in Scripture. He is present in the Word, but I can read the Word and miss Him just as the Pharisees did. I want to attend to His presence in nature. I can walk in nature or sit on my porch looking over my lake and enjoy nature without attending to His presence, or I can sit there in inspired awe of God's grandeur. I want to attend to His presence in my conversations. Where is the Father working, moving, speaking, and interacting with us as we talk? I want to attend to His presence in silence. I can be in silence and rest, and it is good for my soul. I need to draw from His strength.

God is always present. But we are not always aware of His presence; we are not always attentive to His presence—even when doing spiritual things. I haven't mastered this, but I am growing in it. I long to get to the place where Brother Lawrence and Frank Laubach were so that I can be constantly living in the awareness of His presence all the time.

Third: Willing Persistence

Third, our attitude in pursuing intimacy with God must be one of willing persistence. Prayer can be difficult. Coming after God is hard. Pursuing His face is even harder. It is easy to slip into a rut and become religious. It is hard to pursue the face of God with persistence. There are dry spells and hard places. Getting alone with God is sometimes just plain lonely. There is often an emptiness associated with pursuit. Even when I feel His presence, sometimes I still feel this emptiness inside. It is actually a homesickness; I feel homesick for Heaven. And if you've ever felt homesick, it doesn't feel good. It is good in one sense; it means we have someplace to call home, someone who welcomes us, loves us, and is waiting for us. What it symbolizes is rich and meaningful, but the feeling here on earth—well, it isn't pleasant.

> It is easy to slip into a rut and become religious. It is hard to pursue the face of God with persistence. There are dry spells and hard places.

Too often we come after God for intimacy, and it gets hard. It gets boring or lonely or empty. And we quit. Or we fall back into religious pursuit, checking off our religious duties. Focused pursuit of His face involves intensity. If we are going to pursue God's face we will have to press in and press through. Sometimes we pursue God because we are desperate, but when we get a little relief, we quit pursuing. We have the wrong goal; our goal is to feel better. As long as our goal is to feel better, we will stop short of the prize. Our goal has to be Himself, not His gifts, not His benefits, and definitely not our feelings.

We will have to persist in this pursuit, for God can appear elusive at times. I regularly spend time alone with God in silence—it is one of my major pathways to pursue God's face—but there are plenty of times when I am in silence and I can't quiet my thoughts. My mind is racing, and I can't focus distinctly and clearly on God's presence for long. I can spend fifteen minutes in silence and the whole time I am battling with a steady stream of interrupting thoughts—but still, I persist. The next day I may find myself in His uninterrupted presence for five, ten, or fifteen minutes and my soul is refreshed. Other times I spend time in silence, and I am not battling interrupting thoughts, but I can't access His presence and stay there. It is an intermittent flow of His presence. Willing persistence is an essential attitude for the passionate pursuer of intimacy with God.

The first night I stayed up through the night to pursue God, I mostly just lost a night of sleep. Not much happened. Tommy and another friend, David, stayed up with me through the night. In the morning, David asked, "Why did we do this? Nothing happened." I said, "Because He is worth it." That's why we pursue. He is worth it. It comes down to just that. He is worth pursuing when He shows up, and even when He doesn't show up like we hoped He would, like we wanted Him to, like we longed for, He is still worth it. We don't pursue God's face for His benefits; we pursue God's face for Himself.

Mother Teresa once went through a very long, dry season of a dark night of the soul where the presence of God was nowhere to be felt. She wrote in her journal, "Though I never feel you again, I will seek to love you like you have never been loved before." When I heard that the first time, I wept. It still moves me deeply. He really is worth it. Do you think you will ever get to Heaven and regret that you pursued God too much?

> He really is worth it. Do you think you will ever get to Heaven and regret that you pursued God too much?

There is a world of difference between wishing and wanting. Many people wish they were closer to God. They wish they had the abundant life. They wish they would hear His voice with greater clarity and regularity; they wish they would know the revelation of His love and experience the reality of His presence. But they do not want it enough to pay the price to draw near, remove blocks, and obtain the treasure. If we are going to go deeper with God in intimacy, if we are going to become face-to-face friends with God, then we must pursue at any cost.

Part of persistence is the willingness to try different pathways to God. Sometimes I am worshiping passionately and connecting deeply, but there have been other times when I am worshiping and I just can't connect with God through that path. There are times I have connected with God deeply in silence, and there are times I cannot. It feels lifeless. There are times I connect deeply with God in meditation or studying Scripture, and there are seasons where I turn to the Bible but it is dry. Still, I don't quit. I try new paths, new spiritual disciplines. I keep coming after God whether I am connecting or not.

One of my all-time favorite passages is Luke 11:13. Jesus says, "If you then, though you are evil, know how to give good gifts to your children, how much more will your Father in heaven give the Holy Spirit to those who ask him!" But the context is: "Ask and it will be given to you; seek and you will find; knock and the door will be opened to you. For everyone who asks receives; those who seek find; and to those who knock, the door will be opened" (Luke 11:9, 10). You can have as much of God as you want, but no more than you are willing to pay the price for. There is always more of God to be experienced, discovered, and revealed. Willing persistence is the key.

I have heard people teach that you receive all of God that you can at your conversion. There isn't any more, they say; you can never experience any more of God. I get what they are saying: you didn't receive part of the Holy Spirit at that time; you received all that you can receive at conversion. But though we receive the Spirit at conversion, we aren't always operating in the fullness of the Spirit's presence. In this passage Jesus teaches the disciples that they can pursue and receive more. That's exactly what happened to the disciples as the story unfolds in the New Testament. In John 20 Jesus breathed on the disciples and said, "Receive the Holy Spirit." In his book *Joy Unspeakable*, Martyn Lloyd-Jones says this was their moment of regeneration.[7]

In Acts 1, Jesus told His disciples to wait in Jerusalem for the baptism of the Spirit. They waited and were constantly in prayer (Acts 1:14). Then, in Acts 2, God answered; they were filled with the Spirit. But there was more: this was an *outpouring* of the Spirit. The disciples experienced a fresh encounter with the Spirit, a new revelation, a distinct experience, a different empowerment. And there was immediate fruit, both in preaching and in power for healing (Acts 2 and 3). But they still weren't done; there was more. They were threatened with persecution because they were boldly preaching Jesus, and once again they went to the Lord in prayer (Acts 4). They were filled with the Spirit a second time—same followers, but new experience, new encounter, fresh outpouring of the Spirit. God is infinite, and there is always more of God to be encountered and experienced. But Jesus told us we must ask, seek, and knock. We must come with willing persistence.

> God is infinite, and there is always more of God to be encountered and experienced.

Authority Expanded in Intimacy

We cannot become satisfied with our current level of experience, intimacy, and depth with God. We must come for more. When my hunger for God starts to wane, I need to find ways to ignite that need. The more I hunger for His presence, the more I will be willing to pay the price and pursue.

When I discovered that I needed to seek the Lord's face to expand authority, I went after God with all my heart. I went on a long fast. I started doing night watches. I continued bimonthly retreat times away with the Lord to pursue His face. At first, there was a clear and definite increase in His presence. I experienced some new revelation, new experiences with the

Lord; there were definite times of refreshing in the Lord (Acts 3:20). I went to Alliance Theological Seminary one weekend to teach a class with my friend Martin Sanders. We were doing a ministry time in the class and I went to pray for his wife, Dianna. At the time (because I was practicing entering His presence), I started praying for people without words. I had become more keenly aware that my words didn't have any power; the power was in His presence. So rather than praying with words over people, often I would just lay my hands on the person and enter His presence. That's what I did with Dianna.

Martin called me a few days later. He said, "Hey, bud. How are you doing?" Then he asked about my weekend services. He said, "You prayed for Dianna on Saturday." I acknowledged that I had. He asked, "What did you pray for her?" I said, "Nothing." He said, "I know you didn't use words; she told me that. But what were you praying for?" I said, "Nothing." He responded with surprise: "You can't pray *nothing*." I said, "All I did was enter into Jesus' presence while I was with Dianna. Why?" He said, "She felt electricity flowing through her body. She had a powerful encounter with God." I said, "Yeah, I have nothing. That's Jesus." I had been pursuing His presence, and there was a noticeable shift in kingdom activity. Spiritual authority is expanded in intimacy. The closer you get to Jesus, the more of His presence you carry. And the more you carry His presence, the more the kingdom comes.

But there was also a new level of resistance, and there were new attacks. I went through a season where I was criticized severely. The attacks were mostly couched in terms of theology, but the reality was I hadn't changed what I believed. I was simply emphasizing some things more than I used to. My battle was in the heavenly realms, and as I focused on intimacy and revival, the spiritual battle increased.

At one point during that season I went to the monastery on one of my bimonthly retreats. As I processed the attacks that were coming against me, I laid on the monastery floor. I cried out to God: "Why, Lord? Why are these attacks happening? I'm just doing what you told me to do." I was surprised that more people hadn't enthusiastically joined me in my pursuit of revival. I was also surprised by the Lord's response to my question! He said, "I'm answering your prayer." I said, "I don't know what I'm praying, but if you tell me, I promise I'll stop!" The Lord said, "For over a decade you have prayed to me, 'Lord, give me the ability to impart your Spirit like the apostles—*if* my character and intimacy can sustain it.' This is what it takes." I had indeed prayed that prayer.

I longed for revival, and I noticed in Scripture how the movement of God rapidly advanced because the apostles carried the Lord's presence wherever they went, and they laid hands on people and the kingdom came. Sick people were healed, lives were changed, people were filled with the Spirit, and the kingdom advanced. If we are going to have an increase in intimacy that leads to more of His presence in our lives, we need to willingly persist through the darkness. Testing is essential in our pursuit of more of God.

My testing, though, didn't end there. It went from bad to worse, because later I went through my own dark night of the soul. For the first time in my life I had no sense of the presence of God; I only heard His voice when I was doing ministry. In spite of the fact that I could not hear God's voice, nor sense God's presence, I continued to pursue Him. I persisted with prayer, reading Scripture, fasting, night watches, and retreats. Every day I showed up. I fundamentally believe if you do the right things, eventually you'll get the right results. It is not a universal truth; it is more like a proverbial statement. It is just generally the way life works.

Every day I came and spent time alone with God, but every day God felt absent, silent. Still, I kept coming after Him because He is worth it. I knew from reading John of the Cross on the *Dark Night of the Soul* that the purpose of the dark night was purgation—God was doing a deeper work of purging in my soul. Before every new level of intimacy is a fresh level of purging. There is often an emptying before there is a filling. Hebrews 12:14 says, "Without holiness no one will see the Lord." I believe there is an eschatological meaning to this. That is, we must be made righteous through faith in Christ in order to meet God. But I also believe there is an *intimacy* meaning to this passage: we cannot draw nearer to God without growing in holiness. Sin hinders intimacy with God, so God shines His light into the dark places of our soul. God never shines His light into our soul to make us feel bad; He shines His light to get us free, so we can draw nearer still. And one of the ways God grows us up in holiness is through hardship and through the dark night of the soul. I was seeking God's face, but I couldn't see Him without holiness. So I embraced the dark night as a necessary means to the end that both God and I were after: intimacy.

Testing is necessary for holiness to develop. We often think of holiness in terms of things we must not do: don't lust, don't

> Before every new level of intimacy is a fresh level of purging. There is often an emptying before there is a filling. Hebrews 12:14 says, "Without holiness no one will see the Lord."

be greedy, don't envy, etc. But holiness is more about the people we are becoming than it is about the things we stop doing. Holiness is about becoming like Jesus. We become less selfish and more compassionate. We become less greedy and more generous. We become less impatient and more longsuffering. We become less strong-willed and more surrendered. But these traits are most often developed in the fire of testing, trials, difficulties, and suffering. Here is where self dies and Christ is formed in us. We must be willingly persistent in our pursuit so we can empty the suitcase of the self-life and make more room for Jesus to abide in us and us in Him.

After months of silence and absence, one day I sensed the Lord's presence again. It wasn't anything dramatic. It was a gentle reentry of His presence. But immediately I noticed a new level of authority. More people were healed when I prayed for the sick, more people were filled with the Spirit when I prayed for people to be filled, and, as I ministered, more people encountered God's love than ever before. There was more power. There were more answers to prayer; there was a noticeable increase in authority.

But those things wouldn't have come without willing persistence. We must be willing to wade through the darkness. We must persist in pursuit because He is worth it. We are not pursuing His hands, we are pursuing His face. We are not pursuing answers, we are pursuing *Him*.

If we are going to move mountains, we need God. Only God can do the impossible. We must draw near. Authority is rooted in identity, expanded in intimacy, and activated by faith.

In our final chapter, we'll explore faith.

Six:
Activated By Faith

Spiritual authority is rooted in identity, expanded in intimacy, and *activated by faith.*

Faith: It is one of the most important words in the Bible. It is hard to get around it; faith is of utmost importance in our relationship with God. We cannot enter the kingdom of God without faith. Jesus told us the kingdom was at hand and to repent and believe (Mark 1:15). We cannot advance in intimacy with God without faith; we cannot draw near to someone we do not trust deeply. We cannot walk in step with the Spirit without faith. We are going to have to develop a deep-seated, active trust in the goodness of God if we are going to weather the tough seas of the spiritual journey and continue to grow closer to God through the storms. We cannot see the kingdom come with power without faith. There are many things God would love to see happen that do not happen because the people of God do not believe.

Many Christians today are nearly fatalistic in their thinking. People often act as though everything that happens is God's sovereign plan; that is, God has ordained absolutely everything that takes place. But that view of God's sovereignty doesn't take into account human responsibility. Rape, for example, is not God's will. He doesn't ordain it. Rebellious, sinful people make bad choices that God calls evil. Those things are not His plan. When sin entered the planet, so did a pervasive brokenness: injustice, poverty, sickness, death, and natural disasters entered the world. We can trace all the evil in society back to sin at its root. God is so good that He can redeem every dark thing that comes into our lives, and He can use it to make us more like Jesus (Romans 8:28-39), but He doesn't ordain evil. God *triumphs* over evil. To say He ordains everything blames God for evil and confuses the undeniable reality of the goodness of God. To say God triumphs over evil gives us hope in every situation in our lives that is impacted by evil.

Jesus' plan is to overturn the evil effects of sin on the planet. He is in the business of restoring the Kingdom of God to earth. He wants us to participate in the divine overthrow of the "ruler of this age"; He wants us to partner with Him to destroy the works of the devil and advance the kingdom. But that requires faith. Our lack of faith keeps us from acting in authority and hinders the work of the kingdom, just like what happened with the disciples in Matthew 17 when they couldn't drive out the demon from the boy.

Let's talk about how faith works in releasing God's power in Jesus' ministry; how spiritual authority is activated by faith; and then close this discussion on how to develop faith. That last part will explain some key steps for which we are responsible, and God's part in the process of our faith development.

Faith Releases the Activity of God

I want to take a look at faith in the gospel of Matthew and see how it releases the activity of God. In Matthew 8 we find the story of a centurion. He was a man who had a servant who he deeply loved, but that servant was paralyzed and suffering terribly. This military leader approaches Jesus asking for help, and Jesus offers to go with the man to heal his servant. But the centurion stuns Jesus with his response: "Lord, I do not deserve to have you come under my roof. But just say the word, and my servant will be healed. For I myself am a man under authority, with soldiers under me. I tell this one 'Go,' and he goes; and that one 'Come,' and he comes. I say to my servant, 'Do this,' and he does it." And for the first time in the Bible, Jesus is amazed. He is amazed at the man's great faith, saying that He has not seen such great faith anywhere in Israel.

> For the first time in the Bible, Jesus is amazed. He is amazed at the man's great faith, saying that He has not seen such great faith anywhere in Israel.

The centurion understood authority. He was under authority and obeyed commands given to him; he had men who worked under him in the military, and they obeyed his orders. Somehow, the man makes a connection between military authority and spiritual authority. He realizes that just as he has authority over those under him, Jesus has authority over sickness. How did he make that leap? Maybe he had seen Jesus heal others with His word. Maybe he had only heard about Jesus healing other people, or maybe he had listened to Jesus preach about the kingdom of God and then seen Jesus heal, and he put it all together. Jesus is the King of the kingdom, and just as a general has authority over everyone who reports to him, so Jesus has authority over everything in His kingdom realm. He doesn't even need to show up; He can simply make a command and it will happen.

Somehow or other this man gets that, just as he has men in authority above him, Jesus is doing His Father's bidding. And if this Jesus merely speaks the word, the Father will activate that word without Jesus even being present. Jesus has the right to speak on behalf of the Father just as the centurion had the right to speak on behalf of the government and those in authority over him. It is an amazing association, and it leads to immediate and miraculous results. That's faith at its strongest and very best, faith that amazed Jesus at its depth of implication and application. It's faith that activated the Word of God to speak and the hand of God to move on behalf of a servant who wasn't even present when that word was spoken.

Jesus said to the centurion, "Go! Let it be done just as you believed it would. And his servant was healed at that very hour" (Matthew 8:13). It was faith that touched Heaven and changed the outcomes on earth.

Your Faith Has Healed You

Just one chapter later in Matthew we come to another story where faith releases results. Jesus is invited to go with a man to raise his daughter from the dead, and this man too displays great faith: "My daughter just died. But come and put your hand on her, and she will live" (Matthew 9:18). As Jesus is going with him, a woman who had been afflicted with bleeding for twelve years approaches Jesus—but she is stealthy. She doesn't let Jesus know she is in need; she doesn't ask for anything. She just sneaks up on Him and slyly touches the edge of His cloak. "She said to herself, 'If I only touch his cloak, I will be healed.'" Amazing faith: she believed that power would be transferred through merely touching His clothes. She believed she could reach out and appropriate the healing power of Jesus without His even knowing about it.

Mark's version of this same story adds some color. "Immediately her bleeding stopped, and she felt in her body that she was freed from her suffering" (Mark 5:29). Mark proceeds to tell us that Jesus felt power leave His body, and he quickly asked who touched Him. It is a comical moment as the disciples are thinking, "Duh! Are you kidding us? Have you noticed the crowd pressing into us and practically crushing us? Everyone is trying to get a piece of you!" But Jesus persists because He knows some supernatural transfer of power has taken place in response to faith. The woman's faith had been so strong that it released the power of Jesus without even asking Jesus for the miracle or making it known to Him that she needed one! She reached out and grabbed faith, literally; she believed, and it was done for her. That's faith! So Jesus looks for the woman until He finds her. She approached with fear and trembling, but Jesus said to her, "Daughter, *your faith has healed you.* Go in peace and be freed from your suffering" (Mark 5:34, emphasis mine).

> She reached out and grabbed faith, literally; she believed, and it was done for her. That's faith!

Once again, faith activates the power of God to rescue a suffering woman from her physical plight. But there is a subplot to this story that is worth mentioning. The woman wasn't just suffering physically; due to the issue of blood she was also considered unclean in the religious community. She was shunned, a social outcast. This woman was suffering emotionally as well as physically. This is why Jesus calls her out. Mark notes that people regularly touched Jesus in the crowds and were healed. Mark 6:56: "And wherever he went—into villages, towns or countryside—they placed the sick in the marketplaces. They begged him to let them touch even the edge of his cloak, and all who touched him were healed." This was, and is, kingdom normal. Wherever Jesus is present, the power of God is available to appropriate for those who believe.

But this time Jesus stopped, and that alone is noteworthy. It is the only time recorded where Jesus stops and searches for one of these faith-filled garment grabbers. I am sure He felt power leave Him many times, but this time He was drawn to stop and look for her because He must have sensed her healing wasn't complete—because there had been rejection and social ostracism that produced shame, and He wanted to release more than physical healing. He wanted to heal her soul.

> **Faith not only activates healing for what we perceive we need, faith can activate healing for what Jesus perceives we need!**

Faith not only activates healing for what we perceive we need, faith can activate healing for what Jesus perceives we need! He perceives far more than we do. And not to be lost in this story, the faith of the father in this account moved Jesus to act powerfully too. He raised that girl from the dead!

Too often I hear people teach and pray in a way that encourages a resigned, passive faith. "God will do whatever God wants to do." "Whatever God wants will happen." But that is not the faith we see in the gospels. All these people had an active, engaged, participatory faith, and Jesus responded to their faith with more than commendations. He responded with the release of supernatural power. Heaven invaded earth and hell was overturned. Teaching a version of sovereignty that produces a passive faith may make us feel better about the impotent results we are seeing in the church, but it won't help release the kingdom in our midst. I am not saying God isn't sovereign; I believe in the sovereignty of God. But I don't believe that diminishes the need for faith in any way. I am not saying we have the power to name and claim whatever we want to happen. I am not saying there is not mystery in all of this, because there is clearly a mystery to healing and the miraculous. But I am advocating that we need to do our part of the equation—not God's part—and our part is to come with faith. God responds to faith; it is the undeniable testimony of the Bible. There are things that could happen that are not happening when we don't come with faith in our hearts.

According to Your Faith It Will Be Done

In the very next story in Matthew we find Jesus departing after the little girl has been raised from the dead, and as He is walking two blind men start screaming out for Him: "Have mercy on us, Son of David!" When they get to Jesus, He asks them, "Do you believe that I am able to do this?" Jesus asks them for a commitment of their active trust in His capacity to heal. "'Yes, Lord,' they replied. Then He touched their eyes and said, *'According to your faith let it be done to you.'* Their sight was restored" (Matthew 9:28-30, emphasis mine). These men were desperate. Who else could heal them? There were no medical procedures available to them that could restore their sight. If Jesus didn't help them, who would? So they started screaming when they heard Him coming by, and they don't stop their commotion until they get His attention! Desperation is the platform of breakthrough; it breaks us free from all our self-reliance and motivates us to throw ourselves solely on the mercy of God.

> Desperation is the platform of breakthrough; it breaks us free from all our self-reliance and motivates us to throw ourselves solely on the mercy of God.

Why does Jesus ask this question: "Do you believe that I am able to do this?" Does He sniff some doubt? Is He trying to provoke faith? Is He simply curious? Or does He see that their desperation is not merely fueled by faith but also by fear? Is his question simply trying to get them to take their spiritual eyes off of their impossible circumstances and put them on Him alone? Whatever His motivation for asking, faith is the result. And Jesus says to them, "According to your faith let it be done to you." And their sight was restored—but again, according to their faith. Their healing was directly linked to their faith. According to their faith, it would be done. I wonder how many stories never made it to the Gospels because the people weren't wooed out of their fear or unbelief; they were never inspired to activate the power of God through their faith. How many people missed out on what Jesus had for them because they did not believe? We know His hometown missed out on miracles because of its lack of faith; the Gospels record that for us. So, how many others?

We are often uncomfortable asking these questions. We want it to be all on God and have nothing to do with our faith. We want it to be completely up to God's sovereign choices because that takes us off the hook. We can live a powerless Christian life and excuse it easier that way—but I don't see that option available to me in the Gospels. We also don't want to emphasize faith because we are afraid people are going to abuse it with some "name it, claim it" theology, or that other people are going to be disappointed because God didn't come through for them.

I don't have it all figured out; I don't understand how our faith and God's sovereignty work in tandem. But I do know that Jesus calls faith out of me, and that faith is my part of the equation, and I do know that I am only responsible for my part. As uncomfortable as that makes me sometimes, I want to do my part and develop my faith. I would rather trust God for the impossible and be disappointed and have to grieve and process than have a passive, fatalistic faith, see little, and be content with that. This side of Heaven, we will always have disappointment, and we will have to process our grief. We need to have a theology of suffering alongside our theology of power. But to have a theology of suffering without a theology of power is to pervert the gospels.

Apparently, there were some things Jesus would have done but did not do without the cooperating partnership of people's faith

> This side of Heaven, we will always have disappointment, and we will have to process our grief. We need to have a theology of suffering alongside our theology of power.

activating the power of God. With regard to His hometown, Matthew 13:58 records, "And he did not do many miracles there because of their lack of faith." According to your faith let it be done to you—without faith, therefore, sometimes it won't be done to you. Mark 6:5, 6 says of those in Jesus' hometown, "He could not do any miracles there, except lay his hands on a few sick people and heal them. He was amazed at their lack of faith." Mark says, literally, that "he had power to do no miracle there" because of their lack of faith. Their lack of faith kept His power at bay. How tragic is that? And He was amazed at their lack of faith. This is the second—and only other—time Jesus is amazed in the gospels. Jesus is amazed by the centurion's great faith, and He is amazed at his own hometown's lack of faith. The only two times that we find Jesus amazed it is about faith: great faith or no faith. Great faith that activated the power of God amazed Jesus; no faith that kept God's power at bay amazed Jesus. Faith is a conduit for the power of God, and when it is not present, the power of God does not flow freely like it could or should. This is a biblical reality.

We can wrestle with these stories and get angry with God because it seems to depend so much on our faith. You can get angry with me for writing these things and not having the "right theology." We can dismiss it and stubbornly refuse to believe that faith has anything to do with it in spite of the plain teaching of the text. If we do that, we will miss out on things of the kingdom that we could have seen. Or we can realize that faith matters and take responsibility for developing our faith. We can take responsibility without being burdened, shamed, or condemned. That's the path I want.

I may not understand how it all works out. I may not comprehend the exact interchange between God's sovereignty and my faith. But I know faith matters and I know I am responsible for developing my faith, just as I am responsible for developing intimacy and maturity in Christ. I am not responsible for God's part, so I am not going to focus on that. When I get to Heaven, I want to amaze God because of my great faith and not because of my lack of faith. There is no honor in the Kingdom of Heaven for being a skeptic; Heaven honors people of deep faith. That doesn't mean you will always see the results you are trusting God for, but it does mean that trusting God is honorable and releases more power than unbelief ever will. We need to trust God for the miraculous, and we need to trust God when we are disappointed.

If you are reading this and struggling with faith, I do not want you to feel condemned or shamed. My faith, too, has often been weak and wobbly. I have often cried out in desperation, not seen the breakthrough I was looking for, and felt the terrible heartache of disappointment settle into the depths of my soul.

> Process your disappointments. Grieve your heartaches and losses. Repent of your unbelief and wrestle down your doubt. Surrender it all to God and do all you can to develop your faith.

I have no condemnation to offer. I have fought for a deeper faith and seen the benefits, and I can sincerely testify that it is worth the struggle. Process your disappointments. Grieve your heartaches and losses. Repent of your unbelief and wrestle down your doubt. Surrender it all to God and do all you can to develop your faith, because there are things that can be experienced through deep faith that cannot be experienced from the seat of resigned, passive faith.

You Have Great Faith

Beginning in Matthew 15:21 we're told a bewildering story of faith. Jesus enters a pagan region, the cities of Tyre and Sidon, probably to have a form of retreat with His disciples. But once again He is discovered, this time by a Canaanite woman in desperate need. Her daughter is demonized and suffering terribly. Literally, this little girl is cruelly demonized. When the mother cried out to Jesus, He ignores her. Surprisingly, Jesus didn't say a word. The disciples found her annoying, so they wanted Jesus to do something to get rid of her. But Jesus says, "I was sent only to the lost sheep of Israel." The woman was irrepressible; she knelt before Jesus and begged for help. Jesus finally spoke to her: "It is not right to take the children's bread and toss it to the dogs."

This is an uncharacteristically cold response from Jesus. Consider: when Jesus does something that seems totally out of character for Him, you have to pause and ask why. In this case, I suspect it was because Jesus was trying to address the prejudice in His disciples. His ignoring her, followed by His response about the children's bread and the dogs, made this event all the more memorable and the point all the clearer when the breakthrough came. She responded, "Yes, it is, Lord. Even the dogs eat the crumbs

> Wow! What a shamelessly audacious response. Her desperation for her daughter, coupled with her certainty in the goodness and kindness of Jesus, made her shamelessly audacious.

that fall from their master's table." Wow! What a shamelessly audacious response. Her desperation for her daughter, coupled with her certainty in the goodness and kindness of Jesus, made her shamelessly audacious. She actually corrects Jesus! "Yes, it is," she says. And He loves it! "Woman, you have great faith! Your request is granted." I suspect Jesus broke out in a huge grin with her reply. He was demonstrating to the disciples that there were no lower-level "dogs" in God's eyes, that faith can move God's hands with breakthrough compassion no matter how down and out or how needy you are, no matter what you have done or what has been done to you, no matter what color your skin is or what language you speak. No one is beyond the Father's gracious touch. *Faith, born in desperation, reaches the tender heart of the Father and often releases the power of God to the needy.* God loves responding to the cry of the brokenhearted soul who is resting on His goodness with determined faith.

One last story about faith from Matthew's gospel. Let's turn to Matthew 21:18-22. Jesus is about to go to the cross. He was headed to Jerusalem one day and saw a fig tree; there was no fruit on it. Jesus cursed the tree: "May you never bear fruit again!" According to Matthew's account, immediately the tree withered. The disciples were shocked and asked Jesus, "How did the fig tree wither so quickly?" Jesus answered, "Truly, I tell you, if you have faith and do not doubt, not only can you do what was done to the fig tree, but also you can say to this mountain, 'Go, throw yourself into the sea,' and it will be done. If you believe, you will receive whatever you ask for in prayer."

This is the same thing Jesus said to them in Matthew 17 in the account of the deliverance after the Transfiguration. He is drilling down on this lesson about faith. He wants His disciples to know they can touch Heaven and change earth; they can move mountains. They can release Heaven's power upon earth's problems—but not without faith. Faith is the necessary currency of the supernatural. Faith is the indispensable commodity for brokering God's power. Faith is the way we activate our spiritual authority. When our faith is underdeveloped, God sometimes withholds His power, just like in Jesus' hometown. We aren't responsible for God's part, but we are wholly responsible for our part.

God partners with His people. He has given us the keys to the kingdom, and He wants us to partner with Him to establish His kingdom rulership on earth as it is in Heaven. But we must believe. We must understand who we are in Christ so we can speak as His sons and daughters on His behalf.

We must seek His face so we have the intimacy to actively trust Him, hear His voice, know His heartbeat, and touch Heaven and change earth. But we must develop our faith so we can activate the power of God in our midst.

Little Faith

Jesus often chides His disciples because of their lack of faith; He knew how important faith was to His kingdom advancement strategy. He knew they couldn't operate in authority without faith, and He needed them to get this. In Matthew 6:30 He chides His listeners for their little faith because they had spent so much time worrying about financial provision.

When I switched jobs from pastoring to a seminary professorship, I took a significant salary hit. My salary was cut nearly in half, and I was moving into an area that required about $20,000 more per year to live. For the first time in my life I faced financial fears. Earlier in life I had planted a church, bought my first house, and had my first baby, all in the same month—and I wasn't afraid financially during that time. But this time I was fearful; there was a lot at stake. I was over 50, we had a lot more bills, I had three kids in college and one more to go, we weren't ready for retirement, and the years were catching up. This seemed like a really dumb financial decision, and I was feeling the weight of it. I felt fear!

As I waited on the Lord, I sensed the Spirit saying, "You will not need to worry about your finances. You will make more money than you have ever made." I had no proof, I had no evidence, there was no sign, there was no backup plan. There was just the word from the Spirit. I was left with one simple decision: I could either trust Him or not. If I didn't trust Him, fear would rule my heart. So I wrestled down my fear and surrendered, and I chose to trust the word of the Spirit.

I had the words of Jesus in the Sermon on the Mount to hold to as well: "Therefore I tell you, do not worry about your life, what you will eat or drink; or about your body, what you will wear. Is not life more important than food, and the body more important than clothes? Look at the birds of the air; they do not sow or reap or store away in barns, and yet your heavenly Father feeds them. Are you not much more valuable than they? Can any of you by worrying add a single hour to your life? And why do you worry about clothes? See how the flowers of the field grow. They do not labor or spin. Yet I tell you that not even Solomon in all his splendor was dressed like one of these. If that is how God clothes the grass of the field, which is here today and tomorrow is thrown into the fire, will he not much more clothe you—*you of little faith?* [emphasis mine]. So do not worry, saying, 'What shall we eat?' or 'What shall we drink?' or 'What shall we wear?' For the pagans run after all these things, and our heavenly Father knows that you need them. But seek first his kingdom and his righteousness, and all these things will be given to you as well. Therefore, do not worry about tomorrow, for tomorrow will worry about itself. Each day has enough trouble of its own" (Matthew 6:25-34). Through this passage, God was telling me clearly: He would take care of me.

After I surrendered, I felt no more financial fear. And true to His word, I ended up making more money that next year of my life than at any other time. Only God.

In Matthew 8 the disciples get caught in a storm. They are experienced fishermen, but the storm is so furious they are terrified. They wake up Jesus, saying, "Lord, save us! We're going to drown!" Jesus replies, "'*You of little faith,* why are you so afraid?'' Then he got up and rebuked the winds and the waves, and it was completely calm" (Matthew 8:23-27). Jesus expects the disciples to trust Him, even in the face of terrifying circumstances. Fear does more to gnaw away at our faith than any other human emotion. This is why the most repeated command in the Bible, by far, is "fear not." We can act on faith or we can act on fear, but we cannot act on both. We must choose. Fear calls us to choose the side of self—self-reliance, self-dependence, self-protection. Faith calls us to choose God's side. Fear puts our eyes on ourselves, our circumstances, our resources, our capacities; faith puts our eyes back on God.

In Matthew 8 Jesus has been preaching about the Kingdom of God; He is the King. The Kingdom of God, and the King of glory, are not going to be taken out by a storm. They should know this, but their fears are often strong and their faith, like mine, is too frequently weak. So, once again, Jesus chides them for their little faith. He wants them—no, He *needs* them—to have a mature faith, a grown-up faith, a robust faith that can carry the weighty kingdom assignment He is entrusting to them. How will they ever be competent warriors of spiritual authority if they have the weak-kneed wobbly faith of spiritual toddlers?

We run into more troubled waters in Matthew 14. This time Jesus has left the disciples alone on the water, buffeted by waves, while He dismissed a large crowd. The disciples couldn't make their way to Jesus because of the strong gusts, so Jesus walks out on the water to get to them. We read these stories so often we miss the wonder of them. Really. Imagine it: Jesus walking on water toward you in a wind so strong that professional fishermen can't control their boat! Jesus is perpetually calm in every storm. It wigged the disciples out, though; this isn't a normal everyday occurrence. People don't walk on water, so they thought they were seeing a ghost. But Jesus says, "Take courage! It is I. Don't be afraid." And Peter, ever the adventurous one, says, "Lord, if it's you, tell me to come to you on the water." What if it *wasn't* Jesus, and the thing *still* called him out onto the water? Hmm. Give Peter credit for courage!

It *was* Jesus, though, fortunately for Peter, and He called Pete out onto the water to walk with Him—and Peter actually did! If only briefly, because then his better senses took hold of him again, and he fearfully slipped under the waves. *Fear always causes us to lose our supernatural footing.* But no worries; Jesus rescued him. And then the rebuke: "You of little faith, why did you doubt?" Seriously? The guy had the courage to trust that it was Jesus and not a ghost, he had the guts to ask Jesus to call him to walk on water while the other eleven are clutching to the side of the boat, and he had the intestinal fortitude to step out on the choppy water that these fishermen could not navigate their boat through! That's pretty

> Fear always causes us to lose our supernatural footing.

gutsy faith from my perspective, but Jesus still chides him for his little faith. Personally, I feel bad for the guy! But do you see the level of expectation Jesus has for their faith? Isn't it a little shocking? Does it convict you a little for your weak faith? It does me.

> Do you see the level of expectation Jesus has for their faith? Isn't it a little shocking? Does it convict you a little for your weak faith? It does me.

Some of you will even feel overwhelmed by it. Don't be! That would make it too much about you and not enough about Jesus. *Faith begins with where we put our spiritual eyes.* Eyes on Jesus. He isn't nervous. If we can keep our eyes on Jesus, our faith can be strengthened. My faith is weakened when I make it too much about me and get my eyes fully on myself. If I am going to develop strong faith, I have to realize when I have weak faith and look to see where I am making it too much about me. I have to deal with my fear, get my eyes on Jesus, and strengthen my weak faith through focused attention on Jesus' unlimited capability. Spiritual authority is not about my power; spiritual authority is the right to use Jesus' power.

Why does Jesus expect their faith to be so strong? Because He was with them. He proved Himself to them over and over. He explained the kingdom to them, and they still weren't getting it, and He was about to leave them. So much was riding on the disciples understanding these kingdom concepts so deeply that their faith could move mountains; that they could grow to a place of touching Heaven to change earth. This is the kingdom of Heaven—this is the supernatural realm of light invading the darkness that has pervaded the natural realm.

This invasion can't happen without faith. This isn't about our best human efforts to create a cool church that can attract people. This is about Heaven bursting on the scene of our sin-stained, evil-tainted, hell-infected planet so the eternal-bound captives can be set free. Faith was needed so the invasion of Heaven could overthrow the reign of hell on earth, that the Kingdom of Heaven could burst through, proving to all who witnessed the outbreak of Heaven in their midst that this Jesus really was King!

Proclamation and Demonstration

The New Testament does not entertain the concept of the proclamation of the gospel of the kingdom without a demonstration of power. The demonstration of power in the physical realm proves that Jesus is the King of the kingdom who has authority over both the spiritual and physical realms. If Jesus is the King of the Kingdom of Heaven, He, by necessity, has authority over both the spiritual and physical realms. In Mark 2 the story is told of the paralyzed man who is lowered through a roof to be brought to Jesus for healing. Jesus sees the faith of the young man and his friends and says, "Son, your sins are forgiven." The religious leaders are annoyed because Jesus, to their thinking, is blaspheming; only God can forgive sins! And they are right about that last part.

Forgiveness is a gift that can only be offered by the offended party; it can never be deserved or earned. Let's say I sin against John by gossiping against him, but I feel bad about it, so I go to my friend Bill and say, "I gossiped against John. I feel really bad. Would you forgive me?" Bill could answer with a yes. But that won't matter; that yes can't restore my relationship with John—only John can forgive me, for my sin is against John.

Sin is a violation against God's glory and His plans for the good of humanity. Therefore, only God can forgive sins; the religious leaders are actually right in their theological reasoning. The only problem is they are wrong about Jesus! He is the Son of God; He is the King of the Kingdom of Heaven. And that gives Jesus authority to forgive sins. But Jesus responded to them by saying, "Which is easier? To say to this paralyzed man, 'Your sins are forgiven'? or to say, 'Get up, take your mat and walk.' But I want you to know that the Son of Man has authority on earth to forgive sins." So He told the man to get up, take his mat and go home, and the man did.

Jesus' power over sickness demonstrated that Jesus had authority to forgive sins. When sin entered the world, the world broke. Sin was the origin of sickness; if you can forgive sin, you can clean up its ill effects, including sickness. If you have power over sin you have power over all the symptomatic expressions of sin. Jesus' power over the fruit of evil (like sickness) demonstrates He has power over the root of the evil—which is sin. There can be no proclamation of the gospel of the kingdom without a demonstration of power that shows that the kingdom has come, that Jesus is the King.

This proclamation with demonstration may be more important today than ever before. We live in a pluralistic, syncretistic society—i.e., there are many different religions practiced today, and people pick and choose different aspects from different religions. It is a religious smorgasbord in which people approach spirituality as if it is a buffet table: take a little from this religion, a little from that one, and a little bit from this other one. *In a pluralistic, syncretistic society where all deities are considered equal, only the unequal display of Jesus' power will convince people of the supremacy of Christ.* In a postmodern, anti-authoritarian society people are not going to be readily convinced by good arguments. We need to use sound reasoning; we don't want to be guilty of shoddy, sloppy thinking. But when God's people move in spiritual authority that is activated by the kind of faith that releases Christ's power in our midst, people will take notice. They will be far more convinced by God's power than by my well-reasoned arguments.

This is what happened in the pluralistic, syncretistic societies in the New Testament like Ephesus and Corinth. Paul wrote to the church in Corinth, "My message and my preaching were not with wise and persuasive words, but with a demonstration of the Spirit's power, so that your faith might not rest on human wisdom, but on God's power" (1 Corinthians 2:4, 5). It isn't that Paul wasn't persuasive or didn't build his case for Jesus on solid reasoning. He knew his listeners needed more than reason; they needed to see it, not just hear it.

> If I persuade you by reason alone, your faith may rest, in part, on my persuasive abilities. But if someone comes along who is more persuasive, you can be swayed in a new direction.

If I persuade you by reason alone, your faith may rest, in part, on my persuasive abilities. But if someone comes along who is more persuasive, you can be swayed in a new direction. If you see the message of the kingdom accompanied with a demonstration of the power of the King, however, you will be convinced that Jesus is that King. He is not merely one among many equal deities; He is Lord of all.

Several times in the past couple of years I have had the opportunity to do a healing evangelism service at a church as part of a Holy Spirit weekend. I try to work with the local church that hosts the weekend to inspire their people to invite friends to come, and I give a message about Jesus, the gospel of the kingdom, and how Jesus comes to restore us body, soul, and Spirit. Twice in the past eighteen months a member invited a nonchurched person to come because the friend had stage 4 cancer. The person had received hopeless reports from the doctor; there was nothing else that could be done for them medically.

In both cases, the person came, we prayed for them, and Jesus healed them. Time has passed, and there is no sign of cancer. Both of these people have come to faith in Christ. There is no need to persuade someone with human words when they have experienced a demonstration of the King's power that restores them to health and frees them from cancer. They are readily convinced. The more the people of God learn how to develop their authority, the more these demonstrations of power can accompany the good news of the kingdom that we proclaim. Of course, this will only be true if we live life on mission and step out in risk-taking faith with our friends, neighbors, and coworkers.

In Matthew 16:8, Jesus chides his "little faith" friends once again. This time he told them to beware of the "yeast" of the Pharisees and Sadducees. They discussed it among themselves and thought, "Maybe He said this because we forgot to bring the bread." He responds, "*You of little faith*, why are you talking among yourselves about having no bread? Do you still not understand? Don't you remember the five loaves for the five thousand, and how many basketfuls you gathered? Or the seven loaves for the four thousand, and how many basketfuls you gathered? How is it that you don't understand that I was not talking to you about bread?" (Matthew 16:8-11, emphasis mine).

Jesus expects that His faithful demonstrations of power and intervention in our lives will produce a faith that carries us through the next crisis that comes our way. If we don't bank-roll our experiences and develop our faith, we are wasting opportunities to grow in our authority. Jesus expects that our past experiences with Him will produce faith for our current problems. And when His past deposits into our faith account do not register as faith for our present and future, He chides us for having so little faith. We do not get any credit in the kingdom for anemic faith; this is not honorable in God's family. The problem is that this kind of underdeveloped, under-attended-to faith cannot activate the power of the kingdom in our midst that can move mountains or release the kingdom for the glory of the King and thus set hell-bound captives free. And the result will be that we are attempting to accomplish spiritual ends by natural means. Jesus doesn't want us to develop faith so our life is less anxious. Jesus wants us to grow in faith so we can develop authority and expand His kingdom so people will know He is King. He wants to demonstrate His Kingship—through you and me. This is why Jesus held them, and us, accountable to nurture the deposits He makes in our lives so we can have a robust faith that activates the kingdom.

The last time Jesus rebukes them for having so little faith begins in Matthew 17:14. This is the account in which Jesus comes down from the Mount of Transfiguration and the disciples cannot cast the demon from the boy. When the father comes to Jesus he says, "I brought the boy to your disciples, but they could not heal him." And Jesus replies to the disciples, "You unbelieving and perverse generation, how long shall I stay with you? How long shall I put up with you?" Then Jesus casts out the demon, and the boy is healed from that moment. *Please note: In Jesus' mind, it is perverse to persist in weak, underdeveloped faith.* This is not said to shame us; it is meant to spur us on to responsible, mature faith.

We cannot afford to passively wait for our faith to suddenly and haphazardly arrive at some mature state. Jesus clearly expects His followers to be responsible for the development of their faith. This is a sobering passage for me. My faith is often weak like theirs. He loves me, even so, but I don't want to live like this. I have worked hard to develop my faith because I don't want to get to Heaven and have Jesus chide me for being one of little faith. Only on earth do I have the opportunity to grow deep faith; when I get to Heaven my faith will be entirely grown up as I come into unhindered communion with the King. Now is the chance to honor God with mature faith, now is the opportunity to be responsible, now is the only chance I will ever get to honor Jesus with my well-developed faith.

> Only on earth do I have the opportunity to grow deep faith; when I get to Heaven my faith will be entirely grown up as I come into unhindered communion with the King.

Later the disciples come to Jesus for a personal coaching session: "Why couldn't we drive it out?" Jesus replied, "Because you have so *little faith.* Truly I tell you, if you have faith as small as a mustard seed, you can say to this mountain, 'Move from here to there,' and it will move. Nothing will be impossible for you." They couldn't cast it out, Jesus said quite simply, because they had so little faith. Little faith doesn't activate spiritual authority that releases the kingdom. Little faith often misses out on the potential for us in our identity and intimacy. Little faith robs us of experiencing the fullness of the promises of God.

Then Jesus doubles down. He pulls out that double truly, saying, in effect: "I know you won't believe it, but I'm telling you, this one you can take the eternal bank of Heaven, and it is double true. If you have faith as small as a mustard seed, you can move mountains. Nothing will be impossible for you." The mustard seed, as you likely know, was the smallest known seed in Jesus' day. Just the tiniest bit of faith in the most powerful One can move mountains. Yet their faith, in Jesus' estimation, was so small it wasn't even mustard seed-worthy.

Our active trust often shrinks beneath mustard seed-sized faith because of our circumstances. Let me take a guess at what likely happened here, and it is probably a pretty educated guess because of my experience in deliverance. The father brought this boy to the disciples. They thought, "We know what we're doing. We can handle this. We've done this before." But the enemy of their souls saw a crack in their armor, and he ramped up the battle. The demons manifested in a huge power display; they likely threw the boy on the ground and he convulsed, and voices may have come out of him that were clearly not human. And the power display of the enemy, the desperation of the circumstance, the pressure of the watching crowds, and the sudden awareness of their own inadequacy made the disciples feel afraid. Fear takes our eyes off of Jesus and puts them on ourselves. When we make it too much about us, we are suddenly left with what we can do, which, according to Jesus, is nothing. And we cannot do the supernatural with our natural abilities. This is one of the enemy's major strategic intents: He wants to make us afraid. He wants to make it too much about us. He wants to take our eyes off of Jesus. *Faith is simply a matter of focusing on Jesus so steadily that our circum-*

stances cannot cause us to lose *perspective.* Our faith is in Jesus, not in our abilities, not in our authority. We access our author-ity because our eyes are on Jesus and we know our circumstances are not too much for Him.

> Faith is simply a matter of focusing on Jesus so steadily that our circumstances cannot cause us to lose perspective.

I've been where the disciples found themselves that day. In the early days when I was doing deliverance, sometimes demons would throw a big display of spiritual power and I would feel intimidated, which was exactly what they wanted me to feel. Fear is a tool of the enemy to keep you from the freedom and fullness of Christ. I was doing a deliverance many years back. It was one of the first ones I had done and one of the most powerful I have encountered even to this day. The first demon to come out of the gate manifested; it raged at me. It was powerful, and I was intimidated and knew, clearly, that I was overmatched. So I commanded the thing to step aside in Jesus' name; that is, I was commanding it to let the guy go so I could speak to him directly without the demon raging. The thing raged at me, "NO!" I said, forcefully, "Step aside in Jesus' name!" It roared back, *"NO!"* I stood my ground, but I was definitely feeling wobbly. "Step aside in Jesus' name!" It bellowed, "What if I don't?" I timidly thought, "Yeah, what if it doesn't? This guy is in big trouble!"

Then I swallowed and ramped down my fear; I took a deep breath and reminded myself of who Jesus was, who I was in Christ, and simply said, "Step aside in Jesus' name." And it did. I had to shift from fear to faith or I could not activate the authority I had in Christ.

This is likely what happened to the disciples that day as well. The enemy always tries to bully us into fearful submission to his evil plans. If we can get our eyes off of ourselves, off of our circumstances, off of our enemy, and onto Jesus, we can activate our authority through our faith.

Developing Faith

The reality is you have spiritual authority because you are in Christ and Christ is in you. You are Christ's ambassadors and you speak on His behalf. You are His body, and you act on His behalf here on earth administrating His kingdom. You are heirs of God and co-heirs with Christ, so you can boldly access the throne of God. You can touch Heaven and change earth. But if you don't hold on to that truth, if you lose sight of it, if it isn't increasingly revealed to your inner being by the Holy Spirit, if fear makes your faith wobble, you will live beneath your potential. Remember: *spiritual authority is rooted in identity.* We must constantly hold on to that truth because the more we know who we are in Christ the stronger our faith will be. It is expanded in intimacy: the closer we draw to God, the more we believe. Spiritual authority is activated by faith; we must intentionally grow and develop our faith to release the treasures of Heaven we have been given access to. I am seeing more of the power of God in my life now than ever before, but this isn't accidental. I realized my faith was weak, especially in certain areas, and I set out to change; I determined to strengthen my wobbly faith. I partnered with God in His desire to make me a man of faith. We cannot do it without God's hand, but many people never develop their faith because they don't do their part.

How do we develop our faith? Let's talk about our part in developing faith, and then let's talk about God's role in the process. I wrote an entire book on this concept, *Deep Faith*. In that book I talk about my journey in the development of faith and I share a lot of practical tools along the way; it wasn't easy, but it was worth the trip. You can refer to that for more help in developing faith, but let me give just a few key concepts in the remainder of this chapter.

Faith and Intimacy with God

First, one of the best ways to develop faith is to increase our level of intimacy with God. The more we know someone who is good and honorable, the more we trust them. Even if we have been betrayed and hurt in life, when we draw close to someone who is trustworthy, and they prove faithful to our trust, we begin to open up our hearts to them. This is true with God.

> The more we know someone who is good and honorable, the more we trust them.

I am a very passionate person. The more passionate you are in life, the more you will be disappointed. The more disappointed you get, the more likely you will take offense at God. When you pray for something with high expectation and it doesn't happen the way you hope, you are likely to get hurt and offended. But when we take offense at God, our hearts close toward Him. We don't trust Him.

There were a lot of things I was praying for with high expectations and, at one point, none of them were coming about even though I had prayed faithfully for them for many years. These were things God had given me specific promises for, and

I was praying and fasting and holding to those promises, but no visible progress was being made—and this lasted for nearly a decade. I found myself accumulating disappointments, and it was damaging my trust with God, so I made a covenant with God that I would no longer take offense against Him. I chose to believe that God is really good, and honorable, and I refused to take offense against Him anymore. I had to process my disappointments, take time to grieve, and surrender to the God of the cross who has proven His goodness. My offense was hindering my trust and disrupting my intimacy. It had to be dealt with.

I ended up developing a slogan that helped me navigate my course in pursuit of God. This is my motto for pursuing God:

Ever grateful; never satisfied; relentlessly pursuing Him for more of Himself; never taking offense.

My motto developed through the years because of the mistakes I made in my pursuit.

That motto has guided me to pursue God for Himself—not for His benefits. *Relentlessly pursuing Him for more of Himself.* I can easily get into the habit of pursuing His hands, not His face. This phrase guides me to look up, to pursue intimacy. And along the way, if I am pursuing God, but I don't get the next great encounter I hoped for, or if He doesn't deliver on a promise the way I think He should or when I think He should, my motto reminds me to be grateful. There are only two times to be grateful: when we feel like it, and when we don't. And when we don't feel like being grateful is precisely when we most need to choose gratitude. God is good, and gratitude reminds me that He is good and can be trusted. Gratitude softens my heart and strengthens my faith.

Another key thing is I don't want to become complacent; there is always more of God to be experienced. So I include the phrase *never satisfied* to remind me to relentlessly pursue His presence. The tension between ever grateful and *never satisfied* helps me to be joyful and peaceful, but also keeps me passionately pursuing or persistently trudging forward through the darkest seasons. But I must remember not to take offense along the journey because God doesn't always think like I do—his ways are not our ways. And that reality is often difficult for us to understand. I have to factor in eternity or life doesn't make sense. And too often my limited view and temporary perspective tempts me take offense at God. So I had to add this phrase: *never taking offense.* That commitment has changed my life.

Draw near. He is good. He is trustworthy. The closer we draw to Him, the more our faith will be active. Don't despise the dark times—the dark times are critically important for developing faith. We must learn how to process them well. We must learn how to trust God in the darkness, in the non-answers, in the hardship, in the dry times when God seems distant if we are going to develop deep faith. Thomas á Kempis wrote, "Now, all our peace in this miserable life is found in humbly enduring suffering rather than in being free from it. He who knows best how to suffer will enjoy the greater peace, because he is the conqueror of himself, the master of the world, a friend of Christ, and an heir of Heaven." There are things God can

> Don't despise the dark times—the dark times are critically important for developing faith. We must learn how to process them well.

accomplish in the darkness that He cannot accomplish in the light. There are things God can develop in us through hardship that He cannot solidify through comfort. There are things God can heal in longsuffering that He cannot heal in immediacy. We don't get to choose *if* we suffer; we only get to choose *how* we suffer.

Suffer wisely, don't take offense, and draw near to God.

Feeding Our Faith

Second, we develop our faith by intentionally feeding our faith. Feeding your faith is like throwing a log on a fire; the log serves as fuel for the fire. You can feed your faith by reading, studying, praying, and meditating on Scripture. When I felt the Lord calling me to preach on revival until it came, I really didn't know what that meant; I had no idea how to fight for revival or preach on revival. I felt completely inadequate for the assignment.

I went away to the monastery and sought the Lord for a path forward. He told me to study Moses because Moses held the key. I discovered that the key was the Lord's presence; I had to seek God's face. I had to press deeper into the presence of God than I had done before. That study changed my life. It changed my pursuit of God; it changed my focus. But it also developed my faith—I had newfound confidence that pursuing God was going to pay off in the capacity to touch Heaven and change earth, just as Moses did. Admittedly, it was a slower process than I hoped it would be, but it was worth the trip and I would gladly do it again. I wouldn't be where I am today without that study of Moses' life. We can feed our faith through studying Scripture—it shows us God's ways and doings—and as we go down the road of those who have gone before us, we trust God to show up for us as He did for them as we use the keys to the kingdom He has revealed to us. Revelation breeds deep, confident faith in our souls. When we do the hard work of pursuing God, and studying Scripture, and revelation comes from the Spirit of God, faith is born in our hearts.

There was another time I was studying spiritual authority and I was captured by this phrase in Ephesians: "heavenly realms." As I saw the five times the phrase occurred (detailed in chapter four of this book), I realized this was a case study in developing spiritual authority. I meditated on those passages for quite some time so the Spirit could take that which I knew in my head and make it known to my heart. When we meditate on Scripture, we often receive revelation from the Spirit. He illuminates the truths of a passage to us. Illumination personalizes truth and deepens our faith. Revelation closes the gap between what we know and how we live. We are often living beneath our knowledge. Meditating on Scripture can put us in a place to receive the revelation we need to close the gap.

Experiences Grow Faith

Third, we feed our faith with experiences. I was talking to a friend this week about deliverance ministries. He was looking for some coaching. He is a missionary in Africa, and he is running into some difficult sorcery spirits. I can give him some insight and wisdom that can help him, but the best way to develop faith that can activate spiritual authority at higher levels is to do hundreds of deliverances with people who have been involved in sorcery in that context. The experience won't be easy; he will often find himself in over his head. But his desperation will cause him to pray and fast and seek God for revelation. God will deliver, and my friend will learn new things that will help people get free. Along with that, the experience will expand his authority.

You too will have to learn, struggle, pray, fast, and wait on God. You will have to utilize the weapons of warfare that are at your disposal. It will be far easier and quicker to call on someone who has already won those battles, who has that experience, and get them to come help you do the deliverance or unlock the closed door before you. You can call for help, but you won't develop authority by watching someone else unlock the door; you won't develop authority by abdicating kingdom opportunities. You only develop authority by doing and by crying out to God for answers when you are out of resources.

I often train people in deliverance, and they get stuck on a hard deliverance. Sometimes they call me looking for a pointer. Other times they call me and want me to come and do it. But if I come and do it, they won't develop authority. I didn't develop authority by abdicating my responsibility to do deliverance and handing over the tough cases to someone else. I developed authority by fighting to get people free. I had to pray and fast and wait on God. Sometimes I would lead a session for two hours and get completely stuck. Then I would say to the person, "We are going to have to pray and fast. We are stuck, and I don't know what to do." We would pray and fast for a couple of days and come back at it the next week and battle again.

Sometimes the Spirit would give me a key during that week that would unlock those shackles and set the captives free; I would receive the precise revelation I needed. Other times I didn't get any revelation during my time of prayer and fasting, and I would come back the next week and the Lord would give me the revelation in the moment and the person would get free. But there were other times the revelation didn't come in prayer and fasting, and it didn't come in the moment, and I battled for a second time, and didn't make much progress the second session either. But I wouldn't quit. I firmly believed that Jesus wanted to get that person free, and that I did not receive a "junior" Holy Spirit. The same Spirit that lived in Christ lived in me, and He would show me what I needed if I persisted. No one develops significant authority without steely resolve.

> The same Spirit that lived in Christ lived in me, and He would show me what I needed if I persisted. No one develops significant authority without steely resolve.

Experience that develops our faith cannot come without persistence and without taking risks. When you venture into new experiences, not all victories will come quickly or easily. The disciples had to wrestle, struggle, and even fail on their way to developing authority. Our path will not be any different.

I am developing authority through persistent faith. Authority isn't developed in a classroom. Authority isn't developed by reading books. Those things are useful; I teach in classrooms, and I write books and have read thousands of books. They are helpful guides. But authority is best developed in hands-on experience, in trying and failing, in figuring it out through persistence, in surrendering to God through darkness and defeat, and in praying and hoping and fighting until victory comes. Authority is developed on the battlefield of the cosmic landscape; it cannot be developed without unsheathing our spiritual sword and plunging into a battle with darkness. It cannot come without injury and wounding, without heartache and loss, without trials and hardship, without persistence and relentlessness. Jesus sent the Twelve to cast out demons and heal the sick, He coached them when they got stuck, and then He sent them back into the battle and left them with His Spirit to fight it out until He returns.

There is no match for developing authority like being in the battle and having to fight for a victory through prayer, fasting, and waiting on God. When the key to the kingdom is handed you by the revelation of the Spirit, and you step out in faith and use that revelatory key, and you see the shackle unlocked and the captive walk free, your authority exponentially grows. Your faith in God is deepened, not just for that battle, but also for the next one. Your resolve is strengthened; your battle readiness is heightened. This is how I developed authority the most—in the battle, not in the classroom.

> It cannot come without injury and wounding, without heartache and loss, without trials and hardship, without persistence and relentlessness.

I cannot tell you how many times someone starts out in the ministry of deliverance or in praying for the sick, and things don't go well, and they quit. They tried, it didn't work, so they think to themselves: *This isn't my ministry. I'm just not cut out for it. It isn't my gifting.* Or even worse, they blame the afflicted person for not having faith or for not doing something right on their end. The road to develop authority is never an easy one. It is an arduous, painful path, full of obstacles, trials, difficulties, and setbacks. Don't quit. When you climb some difficult mountain trail and you reach the top of the mountain and take in the glorious view, you feel the joy of the price you paid. It's worth it.

The Necessity of Risk

Let's cover another aspect of gaining experience. It must be said: one of the keys to feeding our faith is taking risks. Faith-building experiences are risky; experiences that develop our faith are fraught with risk and opportunity for real-world failure. John Wimber, founder of the Vineyard Movement, used to say that God spells faith R-I-S-K.

When I was 25 years old a woman walked into my office with some depression, and when I asked her to tell me her story, she told me she was a former occult practitioner and now was hearing voices. I knew it was demonic, but I had no experience in deliverance; I had never seen a successful deliverance. But you can't develop authority in the barracks; you have to get on the front lines. I dove in—I was over my head and out of my comfort zone—and the Spirit guided and Jesus delivered and the woman was set free. The more we say yes to the risks God presents before us today, the more likely we will say yes to the risks God presents before us tomorrow. I was learning how to walk in the supernatural strength of Jesus with authority.

At the time I planted a church, there was a Sunday I was going to preach a message about healing. I got up that Sunday morning, and as I prayed about the message, I asked the Lord if there was anything He wanted me to change in the message or add to it. I sensed the Lord say that morning, "I just want you to add this one sentence at the end of your message: 'The Lord led me to give this talk today because He wants to heal many people.'" I thought: *Is that really you, Lord? Am I just making this up? I don't want to stand up there and say that if that isn't you. I'll look like a fool. Can you confirm that prompting?* From the Lord: nothing. I waited. Nothing. I went to church and prayed that someone would give me a confirming word. Nothing. All through the worship I waited for a clear word from the Lord. Nothing. I gave the talk, and I was hesitant to add that final sentence, but I took the risk. I obeyed what I sensed the Spirit was saying to me, and I told people that I sensed the Lord wanted me to give this talk because He was going to heal many. It ignited faith in people's hearts and people came down front to be healed. More than a dozen people were healed that morning! But it did not happen without risk.

About fifteen years ago, when I was teaching a Soul Care class, the Lord woke me up in the middle of the night. I sensed the Lord telling me the class was full of demons and that I should do a group test. I had never done that before; I didn't know what I was doing. But I followed the prompting, took a risk, and it changed my life, as I wrote about in chapter five of this book. It dramatically developed my authority—but not without risk.

I started doing Soul Care Conferences around the world, and I was doing group tests with hundreds of people at a time. I began to think I could cast out demons from the front, without doing each deliverance individually. I started praying about it. I fasted over it. One day I took a risk at a conference. I did a group test for spirits like I usually did, and I asked everyone who had demons to stand. I broke off curses and shut shared spirit portals, just like I do with an individual. Then I commanded all demons to leave who had no more ground or access points. And I did another group test: all those who now had a clean test (indicating there were no more demonic spirits) I asked to be seated. Twenty-five percent of the crowd sat down because their demons were gone.

You cannot expand your authority without risk. The more you follow the risks the Spirit leads you to, the more you develop your authority and the greater risks He will lead you into the next time. It would have been foolhardy for me to start off my ministry by doing group deliverances. That would have been a stupid thing to attempt because I hadn't developed that level of authority. But I kept walking in step with the Spirit. I wasn't trying to take more risks than He led me to; I was just trying to do what the Father asked of me, just as Jesus modeled. I wasn't presumptuous, nor was I trying to prove myself. I followed Him as best I could, but as I was faithful to steward the portion of the Spirit He entrusted to me, and faithful to persist in fighting the battles He led me into, my authority developed and I was ready for a bigger battlefield assignment. Risk should follow the leading of the Spirit, not our pride or presumption.

> Just walk in step with the Spirit. After your first week of boot camp, you are not a special forces operative. You cannot develop spiritual authority by walking in pride.

It is incredibly important, due to the danger of sheer pride, not to move into a larger assignment than you are capable of. Just walk in step with the Spirit. After your first week of boot camp, you are not a special forces operative. You cannot develop spiritual authority by walking in pride. You only develop authority to the degree you are in submission to the

King. Pride is an act of rebellion, and you cannot use a tool of the kingdom of darkness to advance the kingdom of light. Authority is the right to use Jesus' power. You cannot use Jesus' power when you are not in submission to the King.

Overcoming Fear

Fourth, if we are going to develop faith, we must surrender fear. Often what keeps us from stepping out in risky faith is our fear. It is often fear that causes us to lose sight of Jesus and put our eyes on ourselves. It is often fear that erodes our faith and immobilizes our authority. It is fear that causes us to hesitate when we should jump in. It is fear that causes opportunities to look like obstacles. Example: the Lord leads us to pray for some person for healing in a mall, and we are afraid. Fear speaks to us: "What will they think? What if nothing happens? I will look like a fool. I will be embarrassed." So before we can take the risk and follow the prompting of the Spirit, we must surrender our fear. I faced fear before my first deliverance, and I faced fear before I gave that word about healing in my Sunday message. I had to surrender the fears in order to act in faith. When we surrender fear and act in faith, and God delivers, our faith expands. When I stepped out in faith, and the woman got free, I was more confident for the next deliverance—confident that God would do it again.

Fear is a tool of the enemy to keep us from the freedom and fullness of God. Sometimes what keeps

Sometimes what keeps us from expanding our authority is fear of the Holy Spirit. Fear of the Spirit is demonic; Jesus is not afraid of the Holy Spirit.

us from expanding our authority is fear of the Holy Spirit. Fear of the Spirit is demonic; Jesus is not afraid of the Holy Spirit. For my first ministry assignment, I was an assistant pastor of a church in Brockton, Massachusetts. I decided to gather the pastors in the city to pray. I went out and knocked on every church door and personally asked the pastor to come join us in prayer for our city. As a result, I knew many pastors from all different theological streams.

I grew up in a Bible-believing, non-charismatic, evangelical church. One day I got a phone call from the Foursquare church down the road, and the pastor invited me to a prayer meeting. She wanted the prophetic intercessors to pray over me. I had to say yes; I was the guy who got all these pastors together in the first place! But I also felt uneasy. After I ended the call with her, I went to God to try to wrestle down that uneasy feeling. What I discovered was fear. I was afraid they were going to reveal the secrets of my heart. Now, ironically, I didn't have any secrets because I had confessed my sin to God, and I had even done a life confession with a friend. Besides that, the purpose of prophecy is to strengthen, comfort, and encourage (1 Corinthians 14). God wasn't trying to shame me. The hard part was I had to admit to myself that I was afraid of the Holy Spirit. I realized this was ridiculous, and I surrendered my fear. I showed up at the prayer meeting, which was way outside of my comfort zone, and I had one of the coolest experiences

> I almost missed out on this incredible experience because of my fear! We can't develop authority if we walk in fear; we have to identify our fears and surrender them.

of my young ministerial life. Those people told me things the Lord had told me, things I had never told another soul. They confirmed things the Lord was calling me to—like writing, and a ministry to fight for renewal. I almost missed out on this incredible experience because of my fear! We can't develop authority if we walk in fear; we have to identify our fears and surrender them.

The first time I ever shared my faith, I had to overcome fear. I had surrendered my life to Christ, I had encountered His love, and I was filled with the Spirit. But I had never talked to nonbelievers about Jesus. I was talking with a good friend one day and I sensed the Holy Spirit urging me to tell him about Jesus and what happened to me when I surrendered my life to Christ. I was afraid. My heart was pounding, my hands were sweating, I was reluctant to do it. But I surrendered my fear and shared my testimony. He listened with interest. And I sensed the Lord with me while I talked about Him. Afterward, an older couple approached me and told me they were listening and praying for me the entire time I was telling my story and talking to my friend about Jesus. It was my first voyage out on the sea of witnessing, and the Lord sent them to pray me through it and encourage me when it was done. That friend ended up coming to Christ some years later. That experience expanded my faith in following the leadings of the Spirit.

Review Your History with God

Fifth, if we are going to develop faith, we need to reflect on our personal history with God. When we take life with God seriously, we develop a catalogue of personal experiences with God. These experiences are like tools in our tool belt to fight the battle against evil. God has given me experiences in my past that can prepare me for the circumstances of my present. When I was going through the first and most difficult marriage struggle with Jen, the Lord said to me one day, "I want you to give me thanks for this." I said, "Lord, there are a lot of things I am grateful for, but this is not among them." He replied, "One day you will be more grateful for this experience than anything that comes into your life. Today, I want you to thank me for this, in faith." So I did.

Soul Care, which has literally helped hundreds of thousands of people around the world—through the book and conferences—emerged only because of that marriage struggle. Through that struggle I learned that God can redeem everything that comes into our lives to make us more like Jesus (Romans 8:28-39). That personal history is what first started giving me confidence to face every dark battle that came into my life. I knew if God redeemed this one, He could redeem the next one.

When my kids hit their teen years, I started praying too many fear-based prayers. "Lord, protect my kids from this." "Protect my kids from that." "Don't let this happen to them." "Don't let that happen to them." One day as I was praying, I heard the Lord say to me, "Do you want your kids to grow up to be weaklings?" I said, "No!" He said, "Good. Neither do I. But if I answered all your prayers for your kids, they would grow up to be weaklings. You are trying to pray out the very things I need to allow in to make them the very people you and I both want them to be. You are fighting against me. How did you get to be a mighty warrior? By me protecting you from all of these things or by facing these things and learning to overcome?" I said, "Clearly, by overcoming." He said, "Stop praying that I protect them from all of this stuff. Pray that I redeem everything that comes into their lives." I should have known that. I learned it in my own life, but I was praying weak, fear-based prayers for my children. That day I started praying faith-based prayers for my kids. My personal history with God enabled me to strengthen my faith for my children's battles.

Seek God's Will

Finally, if we are going to develop faith, we need to seek God's will. 1 John 5:14, 15: "This is the confidence we have in approaching God: that if we ask anything according to his will, he hears us. And if we know that he hears us—whatever we ask—we know that we have what we asked of him." We can always pray with certainty when we pray according to His will. The key is to discover the will of God and take God at His word. And sometimes it isn't that easy to do either. I believe the number one job of a spiritual leader is to discern the mind of Christ. When I was a pastor, I was deeply committed to discerning the mind of Christ in every circumstance. I had good people around me, spiritual people on the staff and board who loved Jesus and were committed to finding and doing the mind of Christ. But we didn't always come to agreement, and we didn't always make the right decision when we did come to agreement about what we thought was the mind of Christ. It is hard to lay down our agenda; it is hard to clear the clutter from our soul and hear from God through perfectly pure motives. It is sometimes hard to hear God—period. So we must be humble and try to keep the suitcase of our soul clear from clutter, our motives pure before the Lord, and our hearts surrendered to Him. It must be our heart's intention to find and do the will of God in every situation. The more consistently we do this, the more we will discover our faith is growing.

When we get a leading of the Spirit and follow it the right way, and it leads us into a God encounter, a divine appointment, a supernatural provision, it builds our confidence to both hear God and trust Him. In 2017 I surrendered my fear of our financial future and trusted the Lord's word about financial provision. When the Lord provided for us in 2018 as He said He would, it increased our faith. When the Lord leads you to go up to someone for the first time and give them a prophetic word, and you do it humbly and lovingly, and it lands and the person meets God, you have greater confidence to follow the next leading of the Spirit.

I just led a prophetic training for a group of people. Someone was there who had never heard God speak, but during the exercise in which they were invited to listen for God's voice on behalf of another, they heard a word from the Lord. It was spot on and ministered deeply to the person to whom they gave the word. But it also ministered to the person who received the word—they knew they had received supernatural insight from the Lord. And that increases one's faith. We have to seek God's will, find it, and then do it. When we have prayed and fasted and are fairly confident that we have God's will, that we have God's promise, we hold on with persistent faith.

I started writing books because I felt the Lord told me to. I had a leading of the Spirit to write when I was just 24. I promised the Lord that I would not open my own doors; I would walk through the doors He opened. The doors opened one by one. One day over a Christmas break I sensed the Lord saying to me, "It is time to write." For fifteen years I had held to that promise that I was called to write; I had waited for that door to open. I had a folder on my computer for book ideas and I wrote down new ideas when they came to me, but I didn't start writing until I sensed the Lord's release. All I did was wait and pray. When the Lord spoke to me that Christmas, I said, "Lord, if that's you, please confirm it." In the next six weeks I had four people give me prophetic words about writing. Not one of them knew of my desire to write or of the word the Lord had given me fifteen years earlier. They were very specific words. I had prayed over those promises about my writing for many years. Seeing it happen has given me greater faith in the rest of God's promises.

Our job is to find the mind of Christ and do it. Our job is to believe God for what He is telling us. Our job is to hold to the promises of God—from His Word and from His Spirit. God's job is to give the leadings and promises. It's also God's job to deliver on them. Our job is to walk through open doors when God provides them. If we do our job, God is pretty good at doing His! We can trust Him.

God's Part in Developing Our Faith

What is God's part in developing our faith? I can't cover everything in this limited space, but there are two specific things that could help our journey that I want to look at in closer detail.

First, God tests us. I know this doesn't seem like a good thing to some of you. But let's examine the concept a little closer. James 1:2-4: "Consider it pure joy, my brothers and sisters, whenever you face trials of many kinds, because you know that the testing of your faith produces perseverance. Let perseverance finish its work so that you may be mature and complete, not lacking anything." The Lord uses trials to test our faith. The purpose of the trial is not to weaken your faith, but, in the end, to strengthen your faith. It often feels like your faith is getting weaker in the trial, but if you persevere, it is strengthened in the end.

No one enjoys hardship; no one welcomes a trial. Most of us didn't like tests in school either. But if you had a good teacher, the purpose of the test was not to trick you or make you fail. The purpose of the test was to help you display mastery of the subject. The purpose of education is not for the

> The purpose of the trial is not to weaken your faith, but, in the end, to strengthen your faith. It often feels like your faith is getting weaker in the trial, but if you persevere, it is strengthened in the end.

teacher to display mastery. Nor is the purpose of education for the teacher to trick or shame the student. The purpose of education is for the teacher to impart his or her mastery to the student. This is why God gives us tests and trials. God is the master teacher. He wants His students to master the art of kingdom life and ministry. And this can't happen without tests. Tests develop faith, and faith is necessary for growing in authority. We have to embrace the tests, not resist them.

There are things I could not learn about myself without pain. There are depths with God I could not get to without suffering. There are relational hurdles I could not overcome without conflict. There are virtues I could not develop without trials. There are aspects of the light of God that I could not experience without the darkness. Yet we often try to pray out the very thing we need to pray through so we can become the very people we want to be. I have learned, and am still learning, to cooperate with the shaping hand of God in the trials of life. I am grateful for all He has taught me in the trials so far.

God has helped me be a cooperative student under the careful tutelage of the Master teacher.

But you can't just go through the trial; James calls us to persevere. Perseverance isn't passive; perseverance involves our cooperation. Perseverance necessitates our active trust. Perseverance requires our wrestling through dark seasons to deep surrender. There are certain depths with God that can only be realized by persevering through pain. There are heights of intimacy with God that can only be discovered by suffering wisely. There are godly character traits that can only be developed through the depths of trial, suffering, and deep surrender. There are many things in my life I would not have chosen, but I would not be who I have become without their untimely and unwelcomed arrival.

I have learned to pray that God will redeem hard things rather than remove them. And I have learned to sit in the presence of God with my pain and persevere to find His redeeming hand at work. Faith in hardship has not been easy to learn, and I have not perfected it, but my history with God proves He is redemptive and beckons me to trust when my soul creaks under the weight of trials.

> There are many things in my life I would not have chosen, but I would not be who I have become without their untimely and unwelcomed arrival.

Nobody plans in pain; yet nobody achieves their destiny without it. Pain is always part of God's plan to fulfill His purpose in our lives. Yet, sadly, we often resist the very thing we need to get to the very place both God and we long to reach.

Why? Why do we resist God's shaping hand so much? Why do we struggle to trust the God of the cross, the suffering servant? He is not a God who sits in luxury and watches us suffer without compassion. He is not some rich potentate who revels in the wealth He gained at the expense of His people. He is the God who entered our suffering, who suffered for us and suffered with us. He was born in a barn in shame and died on a tree in scorn. He left His throne in Heaven to embrace a crown of thorns. He forfeited the praise of angels for the persecution of hateful men. This King of the universe is the God of the cross. This author of life embraced a humiliating death. Suffering is a terrible beauty because Jesus entered into it and redeemed it. He is the God who redeems darkness and turns it into light.

I wish I were further along in meekness and humility so that I was quicker to accept God's plan and embrace the path of pain so necessary for my development. I wish I weren't so slow to trust, and that it wasn't so hard for me to surrender. I have mentioned Fenelon a lot over the years, particularly his book *Let Go*. The reason I have read *Let Go* more than any other book except the Bible is because, in my experience, no one I have ever read understands death to self as the path to life abundant, and to freedom, like Fenelon. No one has ever helped me more to die to self, to humble myself before the Master Teacher, and to surrender, like Fenelon.

When I am dead to self—my self-life, self-centeredness, self-protection, self-promotion, self-defense—I feel free, full, and at peace. When I let go of my wants, needs, desires, and rights and embrace the cross, I discover the life of Christ. I have more peace and feel more freedom. But when my self-life once again awakens within me and my heart cries for its rights, as it sadly often does, I lose my focus on Jesus, and His peace departs as my self-concern rises. This is why I so often read Fenelon. Just a little daily dose of death to self goes a long way toward finding freedom in a selfie generation. Fenelon wrote, "When God is attacking the problem of self in us, he always touches the tenderest spot, that which is fullest of life. . . . Even though this is a most humiliating experience to go through, it is best for you to allow yourself to be humbled. Quietness and peace during humiliation are the manifestations of Jesus in the soul" (Fenelon, *Let Go*, Letter 16).[8]

I have come to realize the only time I am ever miserable in my marriage is when I am making it too much about me. So, if I start to think about my rights, my needs, my desires, my wants, I pick up Fenelon again and read—until I find myself dying to self and experiencing the life of Christ. One night last year Jen and I got into an argument right before bedtime. It was too late to resolve it, so we went to bed. In the morning she went off to work without too many words; she was still angry, and so was I. I was utterly convinced of the rightness of my position. Sometimes we are more concerned with being right than we are with being in a right relationship.

I got up and read a couple pages of Fenelon. I didn't feel like it, but I did it anyway. Rather than rehearsing our argument, or nursing my offense, I chose to give thanks to God for all the good things about my wife because I knew that is what God wanted me to do. After spending ten minutes in thanksgiving, ten minutes dying to self, and ten minutes saying yes to God and no to "my rights," my heart had shifted. I texted Jen and simply apologized for my part of our argument and told her I just spent time giving thanks to God for her and how much I loved her. She immediately texted back and apologized for her part, and we were through the argument in no time. Death to self is critical for maturity. Trials are vital for that surrender.

We must say no to self and yes to God.

> Death to self is critical for maturity. Trials are vital for that surrender. We must say no to self and yes to God.

There is no freedom without surrender. There is no peace without yielding to God. There is no abundant life without death to self. There is no fullness without self-emptying. There is no victory without submission to the King. I wish I were quicker to die to self, quicker to surrender, quicker to trust God's ways. I wish it were less of a struggle to come to these restful places of victory. Nonetheless, I am grateful to the One whose blood purged my sin-stained soul, to the One who is so patient with me. I am grateful for every surrendered moment life has produced through pain. I am grateful for every victory forged in the furnace of trials. I am grateful for every battle won for the death of self and for the life of Christ that has emerged.

James calls us to rejoice in trials. It seems crazy; it is so counterintuitive, and yet it is so *kingdom*. As a result of James' admonition, for many seasons in my life I have given God thanks as a discipline, not because I felt grateful, but because He called me to be grateful in all circumstances, because He called me to rejoice in trials, not because life is good, but because God is good. He is worthy. You don't always feel it in times of darkness, hardship, suffering, trials, and pain. Yet if you keep giving God thanks in the darkness, eventually the light returns and gratitude bubbles over in joy from the deep wells of the Spirit within. There is more to be said for perseverance than we may ever recognize this side of Heaven. If you're in the dark, lift your eyes to the God of the cross, keep giving thanks, keep giving Him access to your heart and soul, keep surrendering, keep dying to self, and one day the light will return and gratitude will flow freely again.

There is more to these trials than just the development of faith and character. Authority emerges on the other side of trials when we respond with surrender. We can only operate in authority to the degree we are in submission to the King. In Matthew 16 Jesus asks the disciples who they think He is, and in an astounding moment of clarity Peter replies, "You are Christ, the Son of the living God." Jesus says that Peter is blessed because this was revealed to him by the Father. He goes on to tell Peter, "On this rock I will build my church, and the gates of death will not overcome it. I give you the keys of the kingdom of heaven; whatever you bind on earth will be bound in heaven, and whatever you loose on earth will be loosed in heaven" (Matthew 16:18, 19). It is an authority passage—Jesus is giving the church the keys to the kingdom—keys that open doors to access Heaven's resources as co-heirs of Christ, keys that unlock chains, that release Heaven on earth. It's a grand moment. They are given access that allows them to bind the enemy and loose Heaven's activity in cooperation with God.

But in the very next scene Jesus tells them that He must die and, after three days, be raised to life. This time, Peter rebukes Jesus. Jesus says, "Get behind me, Satan! You are a stumbling block to me; you do not have in mind the concerns of God, but merely human concerns" (Matthew 16:23). And then Jesus says, "Whoever wants to be my disciple must deny themselves and take up their cross and follow me. For whoever wants to save their life will lose it, but whoever loses their life for me will find it" (Matthew 16:24, 25). Jesus is teaching the disciples that they can only operate in authority to the degree that they are in submission to the King. We operate with His power, not ours, and we must be in submission to His desires, not ours, if we want to operate in authority and access His kingdom power. When we forgo submission, we forfeit authority and opt for human power and control. Trials produce the death to self that is necessary to submit to the King so we can become people of authority. Faith is developed in trials; death to self is deepened in hardship that creates new depths of submission and therefore new levels of authority. Authority is not about trying to get God to perform our desires; spiritual authority is about submitting ourselves to Jesus so thoroughly that our hearts are humbled and captured by His desires. Authority is about enacting His will on earth as it is in Heaven, but we have to bring ourselves into alignment with God to bring His will to fulfillment on earth. We cannot bring God's will to earth without coming into alignment with God's will ourselves.

There is one other aspect of God's role in the development of faith that I want to look at: *his redeeming work.* God redeems the hardship to make us more like Jesus and more faith-filled. James 1 promises that God can redeem hardship, if we persevere, by making us mature and complete, not lacking anything. And in Romans 8 Paul expounds on this truth. Paul writes, beginning in verse 28, "And we know that in all things God works for the good of those who love him, who have been called according to his purpose. For those God foreknew he also predestined to be conformed to the image of his Son, that he might be the firstborn among many brothers and sisters. And those he predestined, he also called; those he called, he also justified; those he justified, he also glorified." God promises to redeem everything that comes into our lives to make us more like Jesus.

Not everything that comes into your life is good. Not everything is a test from God; there are some things that are trials and temptations from the enemy of our souls. There are

In Christ, there is always a path forward, always a sure hope, always a divine solution, always a redemptive ending.

plenty of things that come into our lives—like abuse, divorce, rape, racism, and many, many others—that are evil. We all suffer the ill effects of a fallen world. But God is so good that He can touch the evil of this world and produce good from it. He can redeem it to make us more like Jesus. This is so hopeful. There is no trial God cannot use to make you triumphant. There is no hardship God cannot harness to help you. There is no pain God cannot touch to benefit you. There is no fiery attack of the evil one that cannot be used by God to forge your faith. In Christ, there is always a path forward, always a sure hope, always a divine solution, always a redemptive ending.

Paul ends this chapter with these victorious words: "What, then, shall we say in response to these things? If God is for us, who can be against us? He who did not spare his own Son, but gave him up for us all—how will he not also, along with him, graciously give us all things? Who will bring any charge against those whom God has chosen? It is God who justifies. Who then can condemn? No one. Christ Jesus who died—more than that, who was raised to life—is at the right hand of God and is also interceding for us. Who shall separate us from the love of Christ? Shall trouble or hardship or persecution or famine or nakedness or danger or sword? . . . No, in all these things we are more than conquerors through him who loved us. For I am convinced that neither death nor life, neither angels nor demons, neither the present nor the future, nor any powers, neither height nor depth, nor anything else in all creation, will be able to separate us from the love of God that is in Christ Jesus our Lord" (Romans 8:31-39).

You are inseparably rooted in Christ's love. No one can take that from you. No one can pry you from His strong hands. No one can remove you from His loving bosom. No one can separate you from His eternal grip. No one can hinder you from His ultimate purpose to shape you into His likeness. These trials are mere pathways that can be redeemed by His love for your benefit.

So, we can trust him. We can root ourselves in our identity in Christ. And we can overcome. We can be victorious. We can persevere in our trial, mature in our faith, and develop our authority. We can benefit from the darkness to become ambassadors of the light.

CONCLUSION

When I was in high school, I had a teacher who could not control the classroom. It was sheer pandemonium. Kids talked out loud while she was teaching. The room would get so loud that you couldn't pay attention even if you wanted to; there were times I literally could not hear her teaching over the cacophony of sounds. Kids brought little chunks of hardened fired clay from art class and would throw them against the wall when she turned around to write on the board. By the end of the year so many people were involved in throwing the hardened clay that it sounded like a machine gun being fired in the room. There were even a few times when someone threw a chair out the window—and we were on the second floor! (I am not making this up or even exaggerating it!) While the chaos was going on, the teacher would turn around and scream at the class. She had a little notebook in which she would write down the names of the students who weren't behaving so she could report them to the principal.

But nothing ever changed. And this went on every day.

The class got so loud on many days that the teacher from the room next door walked into our class just to quiet us down. He walked in the room and stared at us. He never said a word, but his mere presence and demeanor would immediately quiet the class and all the students would suddenly be on their best behavior. That's authority. It wasn't spiritual authority, but when he entered the room the atmosphere shifted.

Moses had authority. He developed such intimacy with the Father that his prayers changed the outcomes of a battle on earth. He stood down Pharaoh. He overcame sorcerers. He prayed his way to victory against impossible odds. That's authority. When he lingered in God's presence he came out from the tent and his face glowed. His words had weightiness; his prayers touched Heaven and changed earth. He carried the presence of God and the atmosphere around him shifted whenever he arrived.

Jesus had authority. When He spoke people often listened because they could tell His words carried weighty, ancient— even eternal—wisdom. When He spoke, demons listened, sick people were healed, dead people were raised. People exclaimed, "What is this? A new teaching—and with authority! He even gives orders to evil spirits and they obey him" (Mark 1:27). "We have never seen anything like this" (Mark 2:12). Even His disciples, who saw more of His miracles than anyone else, often were baffled by His wonder-working deeds: "They were terrified and asked each other, 'Who is this? Even the wind and the waves obey him'" (Mark 4:41). Jesus is the King. He is incomparable. No one ever carried authority like He did.

Yet it was not Jesus' intention that the miracles would cease, that the power of God would dry up with His departure from the planet. He came to restore what was lost at the fall. He came to inaugurate a kingdom movement. Jesus' coming was only the beginning; it was not the end. Jesus established every victory through His life, death, and resurrection. His intention is to enforce those victories from now until He comes again. And His plan to conquer darkness and overcome hell's tyranny is the church—it is us, you and me. He came to confer on us a kingdom (Luke 22:29, 30). Jesus came to destroy the works of the devil (1 John 3:8) until He returns and consummates every triumph. His plan was not that we "try hard" or "give our best human effort" to overcome an extremely powerful, even supernatural foe. He didn't expect us to outwit, out-strategize, or out-maneuver the enemy. Paul said, "The weapons we fight with are not the weapons of this world. On the contrary, they have divine power to demolish strongholds" (2 Corinthians 10:4). He gave us spiritual authority to battle against a supernatural foe in a cosmic contest. Human machinations are not going to get the job done.

Jesus called us into His family. He gave us His name. He united us with Himself and with His Father. Jesus gave us access to the throne room of the Father, the throne of grace. He deposited His Spirit in us and outfitted us with every spiritual blessing in the heavenly realms. Jesus knew if Satan, sin, and evil were to be undone in this earthly realm, the victory would only come with superior power that came from the superior realm of Heaven. So Jesus gave us authority. He handed us the keys to the kingdom (Matthew 16:19).

Keys open doors. They unlock shackles. They bind handcuffs around criminals and loose people from prisons. Keys give us access to houses, cars, safe deposit boxes, banks, vaults, and valuables. Keys are symbols of authority. Jesus gave us access to the storehouses of Heaven; the riches of God are available to His children to do God's kingdom bidding on this planet. We have access to the Father's heart, the Spirit's presence and power, and the Son's victories, and all because of Jesus. He called us to partner with Him to advance Heaven's reign over hell's dominion. He called us to partner with Him to release the kingdom of light over the tyranny of darkness on earth. Jesus called us to exercise authority in His name, for His glory, to advance His kingdom.

Jesus gave us authority. But too often you and I walk into rooms filled with darkness like that teacher I just wrote about. We are weak and intimidated, fearful, just as she was afraid of her own shadow. She was a nice lady, but she walked into that class every day without any sense of who she was or the authority she had as the teacher. All too often we walk into atmospheres of darkness without any sense of the name we carry, the presence of the Spirit within us, the access we have, or the resources at our disposal. We walk in defeated, not knowing that we hold the keys to victory in our hands. We live as beggars hoping something will shift in the atmosphere, not as sons and daughters of the King of the universe. We pray, pleading for God to intervene, and taking offense with Him when things don't change. We sit around passively, abdicating our responsibility and expecting God to do what He has commissioned and empowered us to do. And all the while we hold the keys to victory in our hands—unaware they have been there the entire time. And so

> Jesus gave us authority. But too often you and I walk into rooms filled with darkness like that teacher I just wrote about. We are weak and intimidated, fearful, just as she was afraid of her own shadow.

we go on living in atmospheres of chaos without much hope that our prayers and presence can change the environment.

That second teacher, though, he knew who he was. He carried authority. He didn't need to use power; he didn't yell or scream or threaten. He just walked in the room and looked at us, and all the rebellion withered at his presence and the atmosphere of the room instantly changed. Isn't that how you want to live your spiritual life?

You have been invited by the King of Heaven to be His ambassador, His son, His daughter, to join Him in His mission. You don't have to take up your assignment. He has given you a choice. But to refuse to develop authority is to choose to walk in powerless Christianity. Why would you choose to live like that, lead like that, when there is so much more?

Don't you want your identity in Christ to be so deeply rooted, so thoroughly sealed by the revelation of the Spirit, that when you walk in a room the demons pay attention and tremble because of Christ in you? Not because you are wonderful or gifted or smart or powerful, but because *you are in Christ* . . . and you know it! Don't you want to be so intimate with God that you can touch Heaven and change earth? Don't you want to carry His presence more heavily so that wherever you go, He moves in power? Don't you want to speak with such faith-filled confidence in God that sickness loses its grip, demons flee, and Heaven invades hell's territory?

> All the rebellion withered at his presence and the atmosphere of the room instantly changed. Isn't that how you want to live your spiritual life?

Not for your honor, but for the glory of Jesus.

I long to see the day when the church will be the church so the world will be saved. I long to see the deaf hear, the mute talk, the lame walk, the demonized delivered, the broken-hearted mended, broken relationships restored, justice served, and the Lord adding to our churches daily those who are being saved. I long for revival, for another great awakening. But it won't happen because we try harder, or because we come up with better plans and better models. We have to develop spiritual authority and partner with God to advance His kingdom!

NOTES

1. Alan Hirsch, *The Forgotten Ways: Reactivating Apostolic Movements* (Grand Rapids, MI: Brazos Press, 2006, 2016), p. 42.

2. Hirsch, *The Forgotten Ways*, p. 16.

3. Hirsch, *The Forgotten Ways*, p. 31.

4. Gary Thomas, *Seeking the Face of God: Strengthen Your Walk with God By Exploring the Faith of Our Spiritual Ancestors* (Nashville: Thomas Nelson, 1994), p. 19.

5. Francois Fenelon, *Let Go: To Get Peace and Real Joy* (New Kensington, PA: Whitaker House, 1973), p. 87.

6. *The Lord of the Rings: The Fellowship of the Ring*, Director: Peter Jackson (New Line Cinema and Wingnut Films), 2001.

7. Martyn Lloyd-Jones, *Joy Unspeakable: Power and Renewal in the Holy Spirit* (Wheaton, IL: Harold Shaw Publishers, 2000), p. 26.

8. Fenelon, *Let Go*, p. 32.

ABOUT THE AUTHOR

Rev. Dr. Rob Reimer was the Founding and Lead Pastor of South Shore Community Church, a church of the Christian and Missionary Alliance in Brockton, Massachusetts until June of 2017 when he followed the call of God to become a full-time professor at Alliance Theological Seminary (ATS) in New York. Under Rob's leadership, what began as a small group of eight believers mobilized on a mission to start a new church, resulting in hundreds of people coming to faith in Christ. Many of the examples and stories from his books come from the lessons learned from planting and leading a church in New England—one of the most unchurched regions in the nation.

In addition to his role as Lead Pastor, Rob is also an accomplished author. His books, *Pathways to the King, River Dwellers*, and *Soul Care*, have sold worldwide.

A gifted preacher and communicator, Rob preached weekly at South Shore Community and is a sought-after speaker. He regularly speaks at conferences, leadership retreats, mission fields, churches, and seminaries in the United States and abroad. His sermons are posted online and accessed by people around the world.

Rob is also an experienced teacher. He is a full-time Professor of Pastoral Theology at Alliance Theological Seminary in Nyack, New York, where he has taught as an adjunct for fifteen years. He teaches Soul Care at the doctoral level and has taught various classes at the masters level, including Personal, Professional, and Theological Foundations for Ministry; Evangelism; Mentoring; Pastoral Methods; Person in Ministry; Soul Care; and Intimacy and Authority.

Rob was ordained as a Minister of the Gospel of Jesus Christ by the Christian and Missionary Alliance in 1993. He earned a bachelor's degree in English from King's College, a Master's of Divinity from Alliance Theological Seminary, and a Doctorate in Preaching from Gordon-Conwell Theological Seminary.

Rob and his wife, Jen, have four children, Danielle, Courtney, Darcy, and Craig.

To learn more, visit www.DrRobReimer.com

ALSO BY ROB REIMER

Soul Care: 7 Transformational Principles for a Healthy Soul

Brokenness grasps for the soul of humanity. We are broken body, soul, and spirit, and we need the healing touch of Jesus. *Soul Care* explores seven principles that are profound healing tools of God: securing your identity, repentance, breaking family sin patterns, forgiving others, healing wounds, overcoming fears, and deliverance.

Dr. Reimer challenges readers to engage in an interactive, roll-up-your-sleeves and get messy process—a journey of self-reflection, Holy Spirit inspiration, deep wrestling, and surrender. It is a process of discovering yourself in true community and discovering God as He pierces through the layers of your heart.

Life change is hard. But these principles, when packaged together and lived out, can lead to lasting transformation, freedom, and a healthy soul. *Soul Care* encourages you to gather a small group of comrades in arms, read and process together, open your souls to one another, access the presence and power of God together, and journey into the freedom and fullness of Christ.

Soul Care DVD Teaching Series

Rob's first video teaching series is an in-depth guide to *Soul Care*. Great for individuals, small groups, or church-wide curriculum, this series will be an invaluable guide to anyone who is going after freedom and fullness in Christ, or endeavoring to lead others along that journey.

River Dwellers: Living in the Fullness of the Spirit

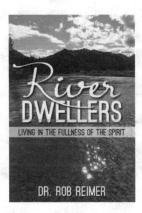

Have you ever wished there was more to your Christian life? Too often the Christian life is reduced to going to church, attending meetings, serving God, and doing devotions. But Jesus promised us abundant life—a deep, intimate, satisfying connection with the living God. How do we access the abundant life that Jesus promised? The key is the presence and life of the Holy Spirit within us.

Jesus said that the Spirit of God flows within us like a river; He is the River of Life. But we need to dwell in the river in order to access the Spirit's fullness.

In this book, Dr. Reimer offers a deep look at life in the Spirit and provides practical strategies for dwelling in the River of Life. Rob explores the fullness of the Spirit, tuning in to the promptings of the Spirit, walking in step with the Spirit, and developing sensitivity to the presence of God in our lives. This resource will guide you toward becoming a full-time river dweller, even during life's most difficult seasons, when the river seems to run low.

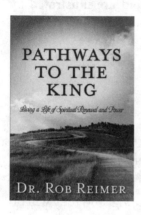

Pathways to the King: Living a Life of Fullness and Power

We need revival. The church in America desperately needs revival. There are pockets of it happening, but we need another Great Awakening. About forty years ago, the church was impacted by the church growth movement. The goal of the movement was to get the church focused on the Great Commission—taking the Good News about Jesus to the entire world. The church was off mission, and the movement was a necessary course correction. But it didn't work. Many people came to Christ as a result of this outreach emphasis, and we can be grateful for that. More churches are now focused on evangelism, helping people come to know Jesus, than they were before the movement. But we have fewer people (by percentage) attending church now than ever before in the history of the United States. We need revival.

This book is about how we can usher in revival and about the price we must pay to experience it. Dr. Reimer believes we have a part to play in seeing the next great spiritual awakening. God wants us to be carriers of His kingdom. He wants us to experience the reality and fullness of His kingdom, and he wants us to expand the kingdom to others, just like Jesus did. To do that, we must follow eight Kingdom Pathways of Spiritual Renewal: Personalizing Our Identity in Christ, Pursuing God, Purifying Ourselves, Praising, Praying Kingdom Prayers, Claiming Promises, Passing the Tests, and Persisting. These eight pathways are discussed in great detail, are securely rooted in biblical truths, and are illustrated by compelling examples from Scripture and from Dr. Reimer's life, the lives of believers in his community, and in the lives of great Christians throughout history.

Deep Faith

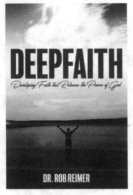

Jesus said, "Very truly I tell you, all who have faith in me will do the works that I have been doing, and they will do even greater things than these" (John 14:12). The extraordinary promise of Jesus is that we can do Kingdom works that He did—cast out demons, heal the sick, save the lost and set the captives free.

Jesus wants to advance his Kingdom through us. But this promise comes with a condition: the level of our Kingdom activity is dependent upon our faith.

There are promises in Heaven that God wants to release, but they cannot be released without faith. There are miracles that God wants to do that cannot be done without faith. There are answers to prayer that God wants to unleash that cannot be unleashed without faith. There are works of the Kingdom that God wants to accomplish that cannot be accomplished unless the people of God develop deeper faith. But there is hope for all of us, because faith can be developed.

Faith opens doors and creates opportunities for accessing God's power against all odds. Faith is a difference maker, a future shaper, a bondage breaker, a Kingdom mover. In his latest book, Dr. Rob Reimer challenges readers to develop deep faith that can release the works of the Kingdom. Faith is not static; it is dynamic. We can and must take an intentional path toward developing our faith if we want to see the works of the Kingdom in greater measure.